CSET Multiple Subject Test Prep 2024-2025

Mastering the CSET Exam with Comprehensive Study Material, Proven Strategies, Full-Length Practice Tests with Detailed Answer Explanations, and Expert Tips for the California Subject Examinations

Test Treasure Publication

Copyright

All content, materials, and publications available on this website and through Test Treasure Publication's products, including but not limited to, study guides, flashcards, online materials, videos, graphics, logos, and text, are the property of Test Treasure Publication and are protected by United States and international copyright laws.

Copyright © 2024-2025 Test Treasure Publication. All rights reserved.

No part of these publications may be reproduced, distributed, or transmitted in any form or by any means, including photocopying, recording, or other electronic or mechanical methods, without the prior written permission of the publisher, except in the case of brief quotations embodied in critical reviews and certain other noncommercial uses permitted by copyright law.

Permissions

For permission requests, please write to the publisher, addressed "Attention: Permissions Coordinator," at the address below:

Test Treasure Publication

Email: support@testtreasure.com

Website: www.testtreasure.com

Unauthorized use or duplication of this material without express and written permission from this site's owner and/or author is strictly prohibited. Excerpts and links may be used, provided that full and clear credit is given to Test Treasure Publication with appropriate and specific direction to the original content.

Trademarks

All trademarks, service marks, and trade names used within this website and Test Treasure Publication's products are proprietary to Test Treasure Publication or other respective owners that have granted Test Treasure Publication the right and license to use such intellectual property.

Disclaimer

While every effort has been made to ensure the accuracy and completeness of the information contained in our products, Test Treasure Publication assumes no responsibility for errors, omissions, or contradictory interpretation of the subject matter herein. All information is provided "as is" without warranty of any kind.

Governing Law

This website is controlled by Test Treasure Publication from our offices located in the state of California, USA. It can be accessed by most countries around the world. As each country has laws that may differ from those of California, by accessing our website, you agree that the statutes and laws of California, without regard to the conflict of laws and the United Nations Convention on the International Sales of Goods, will apply to all matters relating to the use of this website and the purchase of any products or services through this site.

CONTENTS

Introduction	1
Brief Overview of the CSET Exam and Its Importance	4
Detailed Content Review	6
Study Schedules And Planning Advice	9
Frequently Asked Questions	12
Section 1: Reading, Language, and Literature	15
Section 2: History and Social Science	20
Section 3: Mathematics	26
Section 4: Science	34
Section 5: Physical Education and Human Development	40
Section 6: Visual and Performing Arts	44
7.1 Full-Length Practice Test 1	48
7.2 Answer Sheet - Practice Test 1	83
8.1 Full-Length Practice Test 2	97
8.2 Answer Sheet - Practice Test 2	132
Test-Taking Strategies	146
Additional Resources	149
Explore Our Range of Study Guides	152

INTRODUCTION

Welcome to the "CSET Study Guide 2024-2025: Master the California Subject Examinations for Teachers with In-Depth Content, Full-Length Practice Tests, and Proven Test Strategies For CSET Multiple Subject Test Prep." We're thrilled to embark on this educational journey with you—a journey that holds the key to unlocking your potential as a future educator in the vibrant state of California.

Navigating the Path to Success:

Becoming a teacher is a noble pursuit, a journey that shapes not only your career but also the lives of countless students you'll inspire. The California Subject Examinations for Teachers (CSET) Exam is your gateway to this transformative journey. As you stand at the crossroads of your teaching aspirations, this comprehensive study guide is your steadfast companion—a beacon illuminating your path to excellence.

Your Personalized Approach:

At Test Treasure Publication, we understand that success is as unique as each student. That's why this study guide transcends mere preparation; it's a personalized roadmap tailored to your needs. Whether you're diving into Reading, Language, and Literature, exploring the intricacies of Mathematics, or unraveling the mysteries of Science, each section is meticulously crafted to empower you with the knowledge and confidence to conquer the CSET exams.

Empowering Your Journey:

This guide is more than just a compilation of facts—it's a mentor, a guide, and a source of inspiration. Alongside detailed content reviews, you'll find study schedules and planning advice to keep you on track. As you peruse the frequently asked questions, you'll discover the clarity you seek. Unveil the power of test-taking strategies that have been proven time and again, and explore recommended online resources and academic materials that enrich your learning experience.

The Promise of Success:

Inside these pages, you'll find not just information, but motivation. We believe in your potential, your dreams, and your ability to make a lasting impact in the lives of students. As you read our final words of encouragement, envision yourself stepping into the classroom with confidence, knowledge, and a heart brimming with dedication.

Practical Application:

To help you gauge your progress and fine-tune your skills, we present two full-length practice tests with 100 questions each. These practice tests are accompanied by detailed answer explanations, guiding you through the rationale behind each correct response. Your journey from preparation to success is fortified by each question you conquer.

Embark on the Journey:

As you delve into the pages of this guide, remember that you're not alone. The Test Treasure Publication family is here to support you, offering insights, expertise, and a unwavering belief in your potential. With every turn of the page, you're one step closer to becoming the educator you've aspired to be—one who enriches minds, shapes futures, and leaves an indelible mark.

The path to becoming a teacher is paved with determination, knowledge, and guidance. Let this study guide illuminate your way and empower you to master the California Subject Examinations for Teachers. The journey begins now. Let's embark on it together.

Brief Overview of the CSET Exam and Its Importance

The California Subject Examinations for Teachers (CSET) Exam is a pivotal step on your journey to becoming an educator in the diverse and dynamic landscape of California's K-12 schools. This comprehensive exam series assesses your mastery of subject-specific knowledge and teaching expertise, ensuring you're well-prepared to make a meaningful impact in the lives of your future students.

Exam Pattern and Structure:

The CSET Exam is designed to cover a wide range of subjects to match the diverse array of teaching specialties. Each subject is divided into separate subtests, focusing on specific domains within that subject area. For example, if you're preparing to teach multiple subjects, you'll likely encounter subtests covering Reading, Language, and Literature; History and Social Science; Mathematics; Science; and more.

Number of Questions and Time Allocation:

The number of questions and the time allocated for each subtest can vary. On average, each subtest consists of approximately 40 to 60 multiple-choice questions and a few constructed-response or short-answer questions. The total time for each subtest typically ranges from 2 to 4 hours, giving you the opportunity to demonstrate your depth of knowledge and proficiency in your chosen subject area.

Scoring and Passing Score:

Scoring for the CSET Exam is based on a scaled score ranging from 100 to 300. Each subtest is scored separately, and the passing score varies depending on the specific subtest and subject area. It's crucial to meet the designated passing score for each subtest you take in order to earn your CSET certification.

Administered By:

The CSET Exam is administered by the California Commission on Teacher Credentialing (CTC), the state agency responsible for setting and maintaining high standards for the preparation and certification of teachers. The CTC ensures that educators possess the knowledge and skills necessary to provide quality education to California's diverse student population.

Importance of the CSET Exam:

The CSET Exam holds immense significance as it serves as a crucial determinant of your readiness to teach in California's classrooms. By passing the CSET Exam, you demonstrate your proficiency in your chosen subject area and your ability to effectively convey that knowledge to your future students. Your success on the CSET Exam not only reflects your dedication to your teaching career but also directly impacts your eligibility to earn a teaching credential and embark on a rewarding path as an educator.

As you navigate the intricacies of the CSET Exam, remember that this is more than just an assessment—it's an opportunity to showcase your expertise, passion, and commitment to nurturing the next generation of learners. Through rigorous preparation and a deep understanding of the exam's structure, you're equipping yourself with the tools needed to make a lasting impact in the lives of your future students.

Detailed Content Review

This section of the "CSET Study Guide 2024-2025" is your gateway to mastering the diverse subject areas covered by the California Subject Examinations for Teachers. With an unwavering commitment to providing in-depth and comprehensive coverage, we've meticulously crafted each content review to empower you with the knowledge and confidence needed to excel on the exam.

Reading, Language, and Literature:

Dive into the realm of literature analysis, language development, and effective communication. Explore essential literary concepts, dissect textual elements, and enhance your skills in understanding and interpreting various literary works. Uncover strategies to foster language proficiency and literacy in your future students, equipping them with the tools to become lifelong learners.

History and Social Science:

Immerse yourself in the rich tapestry of history and society. Navigate through the timelines of civilizations, revolutions, and cultural shifts. Delve into the complexities of governance, economics, and societal structures. Our content review guides you through the key historical events, significant figures, and foundational principles that shape the social fabric.

Mathematics:

Unearth the beauty of numbers and mathematical reasoning. From foundational concepts to advanced problem-solving techniques, our comprehensive review ensures you're equipped to teach mathematics with clarity and confidence. Master topics ranging from arithmetic to algebra, geometry to statistics, and discover how to ignite a passion for mathematical exploration in your students.

Science:

Embark on a scientific journey through the realms of life, earth, and physical sciences. Our content review delves into the intricacies of scientific inquiry, principles of biology, geology, chemistry, and physics. Gain insights into cultivating scientific curiosity in your future students, fostering a deep appreciation for the natural world.

Physical Education and Human Development:

Understand the importance of physical well-being and human growth. Explore the fundamentals of physical education, movement, and health promotion. Delve into developmental psychology, uncovering the stages of human growth, cognitive development, and social interactions. Equip yourself with strategies to promote holistic growth and wellness in your future students.

Visual and Performing Arts:

Unleash your creative spirit and embrace the arts as tools for expression and inspiration. Our content review traverses the world of visual and performing arts, from the principles of artistic composition to the power of music, theater, and dance. Discover how to cultivate creativity and aesthetic appreciation, nurturing the artistic potential within each student.

And Much More:

The "CSET Study Guide 2024-2025" goes beyond the subjects listed above. It delves into additional areas, ensuring you're prepared for every facet of the CSET Exam. From effective classroom management to educational philosophy, you'll find insights that encompass the holistic role of an educator.

Study Schedules And Planning Advice

Embarking on the journey to excel in the California Subject Examinations for Teachers requires not only knowledge but also effective planning and strategic preparation. This section of the "CSET Study Guide 2024-2025" is your compass, guiding you through the process of structuring your study schedule, optimizing your learning, and making the most of your preparation time.

Creating Your Study Schedule:

Crafting a study schedule tailored to your individual needs is paramount. Begin by assessing your current commitments, whether it's work, family, or other obligations. Allocate dedicated study blocks, ensuring a balance between different subjects. Break down your preparation into manageable segments, focusing on one subtest or topic at a time. Consistency is key—set aside dedicated time each day to review content, practice, and reinforce your understanding.

Strategic Learning Modules:

Divide your study materials into focused learning modules. Each module should encompass a specific subject or subtest. Within each module, outline the content you'll cover, the practice questions you'll attempt, and any additional resources you'll utilize. By breaking your preparation into modules, you create a sense of accomplishment with each milestone reached.

Practice, Practice, Practice:

Intersperse your content review with regular practice sessions. Engage with the practice questions provided in this guide and seek out additional practice resources. Practice tests serve as invaluable tools for assessing your progress and familiarizing yourself with the exam format. Simulate test conditions to acclimate yourself to the time constraints and enhance your test-taking strategies.

Utilizing Study Aids:

Leverage the detailed content reviews provided earlier in this guide. As you study, refer back to these reviews to reinforce your understanding of key concepts. Make use of mnemonic devices, flashcards, and other memory aids to solidify your knowledge. Engage in active learning techniques, such as summarizing sections in your own words or teaching the material to someone else.

Rest and Reflection:

Recognize the importance of rest and self-care in your study schedule. Adequate sleep, regular breaks, and physical activity contribute to your overall well-being and cognitive performance. Regularly assess your progress and reflect on your strengths and areas that need improvement. Adjust your study schedule as needed based on your evolving understanding of the material.

Seeking Support:

Don't hesitate to reach out for support when needed. Form study groups with fellow CSET exam takers, engage in discussions, and exchange insights. Utilize online forums and resources to connect with others who are on the same journey. Seek guidance from educators, mentors, or tutors who can provide additional perspectives and clarification.

Remember, the journey towards CSET success is both a marathon and a sprint. Your study schedule is your blueprint, guiding you through the intricacies of content review, practice, and test-taking strategies. With each study session, you're one step closer to mastering the material and achieving excellence in the exam. Stay committed, stay focused, and keep your eyes on the transformative impact you're destined to make as an educator.

FREQUENTLY ASKED QUESTIONS

Navigating the path towards CSET success involves understanding the nuances of the exam, its structure, and the strategies that lead to excellence. In this section, we address some of the most common questions that arise as you prepare for the California Subject Examinations for Teachers.

Q: What is the format of the CSET exam?
A: The CSET exam is typically composed of multiple-choice questions and constructed-response questions. Each subtest covers specific subject areas, and the number of questions and time allotted can vary. Be prepared to demonstrate your subject knowledge and analytical skills through these question types.

Q: How should I approach the constructed-response questions?
A: Constructed-response questions require you to provide thoughtful and detailed responses. Start by carefully reading the question and understanding the key points. Organize your response logically, providing clear explanations and examples when necessary. Use precise language to convey your understanding effectively.

Q: What are the passing scores for the CSET exam?
A: The passing scores vary based on the specific subtest and subject area you're taking. It's essential to research the passing scores for the subtests relevant to your teaching credential. Achieving the designated passing score for each subtest is crucial to obtaining your teaching certification.

Q: How should I manage my time during the exam?
A: Time management is vital during the CSET exam. Allocate a specific amount of time for each question, and if you encounter challenging questions, consider flagging them to revisit later. Prioritize questions you're confident about to ensure you maximize your points within the given time frame.

Q: How can I stay motivated during the preparation process?
A: Stay connected to your goals and the impact you aim to make as an educator. Break down your preparation into manageable segments and celebrate each milestone achieved. Join study groups, seek support from peers, and remind yourself of the rewards that come with success.

Q: Are there resources beyond this guide that I should utilize?
A: Absolutely. While this guide is comprehensive, additional resources can complement your preparation. Online practice tests, official CSET materials, and academic textbooks related to your subject areas can provide diverse perspectives and enhance your understanding.

Q: What strategies can I use to tackle multiple-choice questions effectively?
A: Read each question carefully, considering all answer choices before making a selection. Eliminate obviously incorrect answers to narrow down your choices. If you're unsure, use educated guesses and move on to maximize your time.

Q: How do I approach the practice tests included in this guide?
A: Treat the practice tests as simulations of the actual exam. Set aside uninterrupted time to complete them under test conditions. Afterward, review your answers and study the detailed answer explanations provided. This process will help you identify strengths and areas for improvement.

Q: What should I do in the final days leading up to the exam?
A: Focus on reviewing key concepts, rather than attempting to learn new mater-

ial. Revisit your study modules, review your notes, and engage in a final practice test to simulate the exam experience. Prioritize self-care, ensure you're well-rested, and approach the exam day with confidence.

Q: How can I manage test anxiety on the day of the exam?
A: Practice relaxation techniques, such as deep breathing and positive visualization. Arrive at the test center early to familiarize yourself with the environment. Trust in your preparation and remind yourself that you've put in the effort to succeed.

Remember that these questions are just a starting point. If you have specific concerns or uncertainties, don't hesitate to seek guidance from educators, mentors, or fellow test takers. Your journey towards CSET success is a shared one, and by addressing your questions, we aim to provide you with the clarity and confidence needed to excel.

Section 1: Reading, Language, and Literature

Foundations of Reading

Picture this: a world where words on a page come to life, weaving a mesmerizing spell that paints vivid pictures in your mind. It's like magic, I tell you. And it's all waiting for you in the Foundations of Reading section of the CSET Multiple Subject Test. This is your passport to a journey through the heart and soul of language, where you'll decode its secrets and unravel the art of interpretation.

So, imagine this: you open up these sacred pages and find yourself immersed in a step-by-step guide that's been meticulously crafted just for you. And it all starts with the basic building blocks of reading comprehension. We're talking phonological and phonemic awareness, those two trusty pals that hold the key to literacy. Together, we'll dive into the fascinating world of phonics, where every letter and sound has a story to tell. And don't even get me started on syllables – they're like whispered secrets of structure and rhythm.

But listen up, my friend, because reading is more than just sounds. There's a whole world of vocabulary waiting for you to explore. It's like an ancient treasure map, guiding you through the roots, prefixes, and suffixes that make up the backbone of understanding. You'll become a fearless explorer, diving headfirst into the realm of context clues and word relationships. Armed with the power of inference, you'll conquer those mysterious words and unlock their hidden meanings.

But wait, there's more! Your journey doesn't stop there. Have you heard of fluency? It's like a beautiful melody of words, tempting you to dive deeper into its embrace. Together, we'll uncover techniques and strategies to boost your reading speed without sacrificing comprehension. That ticking stopwatch won't control your progress anymore, my friend. We'll show you the poetry of pacing and the symphony of smooth transitions.

And now, my dear reader, we bring you to the pinnacle of your reading adventure: comprehension. This is where words come alive, tickling your intellect and engaging your mind. You'll analyze and evaluate diverse texts, searching for the author's hidden intentions, unearthing hidden themes, and unraveling the complexities of structure and language. With the help of quotes and examples, we'll sharpen your critical thinking skills and get you ready for the challenges that lie ahead.

So, my brave warrior of words, let the Foundations of Reading be your trusted guide on this epic quest for knowledge. At Test Treasure Publication, we believe that every student has the potential to shine and carve their own path to success. Together, we'll unravel the mysteries of language, empower your understanding, and ignite the flames of curiosity within your soul.

So, get ready to embark on this literary adventure, because within these sacred pages, you will uncover the priceless treasure that lies within the foundations of reading. Step forward, my friend, and let your journey into the depths of comprehension begin now.

Analyzing Literary Texts

Understanding a good book goes beyond just reading the words on the page. It's about getting to know the characters, seeing their flaws and transformations, and figuring out what makes them tick. Characters are like the heart of a story, pumping life into the plot.

And then there's the power of imagery. It's like the author takes a paintbrush and creates vivid pictures in our minds. Every carefully chosen word and sensory detail takes us to different worlds and makes our imagination soar. It's like a whole new level of art, where words become a tapestry that awakens our senses and stirs up all kinds of emotions.

Themes are another crucial part of a story. They're the guiding stars that give meaning and depth to the whole thing. Love, loss, courage, despair - these themes connect us to the universal aspects of being human. They make us question ourselves and the world around us, and hopefully lead to some personal growth.

The structure of a book is like the bones holding everything together. We look at how the different parts fit together - the plot, the narrative arcs, the storylines. It's all about how the author manipulates time and space to keep us hooked until the very last page.

And of course, there are all the fancy literary devices that authors use to make their writing resonate and shine. Similes, metaphors, symbolism, foreshadowing - these are the secret ingredients that give a story depth and beauty. They make the words come alive, adding layers of meaning and leaving us wanting more.

When we dive into the world of literature, we have to be open to different interpretations and ready to have some lively debates. It's a vast landscape where imagination knows no bounds. Through our exploration, we'll discover the transformative power of words and gain a deeper appreciation for the beauty and complexity of literature.

So, let's go on this incredible journey together. Let's explore the places where fiction and reality blend, and where studying books becomes a key to wisdom and understanding. At Test Treasure Publication, we'll uncover the mysterious secrets of literature and become true lovers of the written word.

Language and Communication

Welcome to Test Treasure Publication! We get language. We get how it has this crazy power to connect people, to bring ideas to life, and to make everything just a little more interesting. We're not your average study material company. We go beyond the boring grammar rules and the never-ending vocabulary lists. We're here to take you on a journey, to delve into the heart and soul of language and communication.

In our study guides, you'll find a treasure trove of knowledge about the English language. We're talking deep-dives into its origins, how it's evolved over time, and what makes it tick. And look, we didn't stop there. We're not just about the grammar and the punctuation. We're all about exploring how language works in the real world, how it changes our thoughts and perceptions, and how it can touch the hearts of others.

We've crafted every chapter with passion and care. We've cracked the code on effective communication and we're ready to spill the secrets. We'll teach you how to really listen, how to speak with empathy, and how to use those non-verbal cues like a pro. Want to know how to nail a persuasive argument or give a mind-blowing presentation? We've got your back.

But hey, we're not just about words on a page. We know that language is meant to be spoken, to be heard, and that's why we give you plenty of chances to practice your speaking and listening skills. Our study materials are designed to get your brain working, to encourage you to think critically and to let your creativity flow.

And can we talk about how language is a living, breathing thing? It's always changing, my friend. That's why we make sure to include all the latest linguistic trends and developments. We're all about embracing different cultures and dialects. We want you to be ready for any linguistic adventure that comes your way.

Oh, and did we mention our online materials? They're seriously cool. We've got interactive modules that will take you on a multimedia journey. You'll get to hear and see authentic language in action through audio and video clips. You can have virtual conversations, join language forums, and get real-time feedback on your skills. It's like magic, but better.

Here at Test Treasure Publication, we know that language and communication aren't just things you study in the classroom. They're life skills that will take you places. They'll give you the confidence to express yourself, to really connect with others, and to navigate this crazy world we live in. Our study materials are here to ignite that spark in you, to make you fall in love with language and communication like never before.

So let's go on this linguistic adventure together, where we'll turn words into our greatest allies and communication into a bridge that spans minds. At Test Treasure Publication, language and communication aren't just subjects to study – they're keys to personal growth, cultural understanding, and endless possibilities. Are you ready? Let's do this.

Section 2: History and Social Science

World History

Hey there! Have you ever stopped and wondered about the incredible story behind our world? I mean, seriously, there's so much more to history than just boring old dates and facts. It's like this big, epic adventure that takes us on a wild ride through time and across all kinds of different places.

You see, World History is all about unraveling the intricate tapestry of civilizations and cultures that have shaped our world as we know it today. It's like diving deep into the stories of ancient societies and getting to understand their social, political, economic, and cultural systems. And let me tell you, it's a real eye-opener. You start to see how everything that happened in the past has shaped the world we live in now.

I mean, think about it. When we explore the rise and fall of empires, the spread of ideas and religions, and the clash of civilizations, we can't help but be amazed at the indomitable spirit of human resilience. From the mind-blowing wonders of Ancient Egypt to the crazy adventures of the Age of Discovery, from those dramatic moments during the French Revolution to the horrors of World War II, it's like each chapter of history reveals a whole new level of complexity to the human story.

And here's the best part: by studying World History, we can start connecting the dots. We can see patterns, analyze how one thing leads to another, and really get a sense of how historical events have shaped our present-day society. It's like getting to learn from the mistakes and triumphs of those who came before us. That way, we can face the future with a more informed perspective.

As students of World History, we become kind of like time travelers. We get to immerse ourselves in the diverse cultures and struggles of countless generations past. It's filled with tales of heroes and villains, revolutions and evolutions. It's a story that never gets boring, with plenty of thrills and discoveries along the way. I mean, seriously, it's a story that shows just how amazing the human spirit can be.

So, my friend, I invite you to join me on this incredible journey through the annals of World History. We're gonna unravel the mysteries of ancient civilizations, get a front-row seat to everything that shaped our modern world, and dive deep into the depths of human achievement. And hey, as we unravel all these complexities and dig into the nitty-gritty of World History, I hope each chapter lights a fire in your soul. May it challenge you, inspire you, and ignite a lifelong passion for embracing the lessons of the past. Let's embark on this extraordinary odyssey together, where education becomes a gateway to understanding and empathy, and where the past becomes an invaluable guidebook for shaping a brighter future.

United States History

Alright, folks, buckle up and get ready for a wild ride through American history! We're diving deep into the epic tale of the American Revolution, a game-changing period that set our nation on fire for independence. We'll be right there in the thick of things, marching alongside the brave soldiers who fought tooth and nail for liberty. And hey, we're not just skimming the surface here – we're going to dig into the causes, the key events, and the standout figures that shaped this extraordinary chapter.

Now, hold on to your hats, because we're about to meet some incredible minds that laid the groundwork for our great nation. We're talking about the founding fathers, folks. From the visionary leadership of George Washington to the sheer brilliance of Thomas Jefferson's wordsmithing, we're going to uncover the secrets of their genius and unravel the intricacies of the Constitution they built with their own two hands. It was a time of enlightenment, my friends, where democracy was born and the principles we hold dear were formed.

Okay, get ready, because things are about to get even more exciting. We're hitting the trail with the pioneers who embarked on a dangerous journey into the unknown. Guided by Manifest Destiny – that mysterious force driving the expansion of the United States from coast to coast – we'll witness the impact of westward expansion on indigenous peoples. I'm talking untamed wilderness here, waiting for those daring settlers who were just crazy enough to follow the call of destiny.

Now, prepare yourselves for the Civil War, arguably the most intense and tumultuous moment in American history. We're heading to the battlefield, folks, exploring the causes and consequences of this epic clash. With the cries for emancipation echoing through our souls, we'll navigate a complex web of political tension, ideological clashes, and ferocious fights for freedom that ultimately tore our nation apart. Along the way, we'll shine a spotlight on incredible figures like Abraham Lincoln and Frederick Douglass, because their stories are interwoven into the fabric of our country.

As the smoke clears from the war, get ready to step into the glittering era of the Gilded Age. In this section, we're going to peel back the layers of prosperity and expose the harsh truths of economic inequality and corruption festering just beneath the surface. We'll tackle the rise of industrialization, the birth of labor movements, and the fiery spirit of progressive leaders who fought tooth and nail against injustice. It's a transformative era that shaped America's progress, and believe me, it's a story you won't want to miss.

Now, let's stand shoulder to shoulder with the courageous rebels who dared to challenge the status quo and fight for equality in the Civil Rights Movement. We're talking about legends like Rosa Parks, who wouldn't budge from her seat, and the powerful words of Martin Luther King Jr. Brace yourselves as we witness the indomitable spirit that shook the very foundations of our society. We're going to experience pivotal moments like the Montgomery Bus Boycott and the historic March on Washington. Let's dig deep into the struggle for civil rights and honor the remarkable legacy it left behind.

And as we approach the end of our journey, folks, it's time to cast our gaze toward the future. In this final chapter, we're diving into contemporary times to explore the triumphs and challenges that define America today. From the digital revolution to the urgent matters of climate change and immigration, we'll uncover how historical events continue to shape and transform our mighty United States. Together, we'll embrace the responsibility of crafting a brighter future and cement our understanding of the invaluable lessons learned from the past.

So, grab your backpacks, folks, because we're embarking on an extraordinary adventure through United States history. We're unlocking the secrets of the past, paving the way for a better tomorrow. The pages of history are spread out before us, just waiting to be explored, analyzed, and truly understood. Let's not keep them waiting any longer – let the journey begin!

Civics and Government

Hey there! Are you ready to embark on an extraordinary journey of exploration and discovery with me? Together, hand in hand, we'll unlock the mysteries of Civics and Government. Trust me, this won't be your average study guide. We're gonna dig deep into the complexities of the American government, unraveling its foundations and evolution throughout history. Buckle up, my friend, 'cause this is gonna be a wild ride!

We won't leave any stone unturned as we dive into the roles and functions of each branch of government. We'll be exploring the powers of the executive, the legislative, and the judicial branches, and trust me, they each have their unique responsibilities. But here's the kicker - we'll also be diving into the juicy stuff. We'll be talking about the system of checks and balances that ensures the preservation of liberty. It's like a suspenseful game, where one branch keeps the others in check. You won't believe the drama that goes on behind the scenes!

Oh, but it's not all about facts and figures. Nope, we go beyond that. We're gonna get into the nitty-gritty of the principles and ideals that underpin our democracy. You know, the stuff that gets you thinking about your place in society. We'll be exploring the concept of civic participation, discussing the rights and responsibilities of citizens, and let's not forget the importance of being an active participant in our democracy. Voting, my friend, it matters. It's like shaping the policies that directly affect our lives - now that's some power.

But hold on tight, 'cause we're just getting started. Let's dive into the murky waters of political parties and ideologies. Trust me, it's a jungle out there. We'll dissect the nuances of it all, helping you navigate the political landscape and make informed decisions. This isn't about just picking a side - it's about understanding the complexities and making your voice heard in the democratic process.

And guess what? We won't be skipping the good stuff. We'll be delving into the Constitution and the Bill of Rights - the backbone of our freedoms. This is where things get really interesting. We'll be dissecting the amendments that protect our rights and ensure equal treatment for all. But wait, there's more! We'll dig into landmark Supreme Court cases that have reshaped how we interpret these rights. The debates and controversies surrounding them? You won't be able to look away.

Now, I won't stop there. Oh no, my friend. We'll be challenging your critical thinking skills with thought-provoking questions and engaging activities. This isn't about regurgitating information. Nope, it's about applying your newfound knowledge to real-world situations. We want you to fully understand how government affects your everyday life. We're in this together, shaping a future that reflects your values and aspirations.

So, are you ready to join me? It's not just a study guide. It's a journey to knowledge, understanding, and meaningful change. Let's make sure you're equipped with the knowledge and skills you need to be an active participant in the political process. Together, we'll light that spark of passion for learning and empower you to make a difference in the world. Because an informed and engaged citizenry is what makes our democracy thrive. Let's go, my friend. Adventure awaits!

Section 3: Mathematics

Arithmetic and Basic Operations

Let's start by talking about arithmetic and why it actually matters in our lives. Arithmetic, at its core, is all about crunching numbers and doing calculations, like adding, subtracting, multiplying, and dividing. It might sound basic, but trust me, these are the fundamental building blocks for all the fancy math stuff that comes later. And when you think about it, we use arithmetic all the time in our day-to-day lives, whether it's figuring out how much money we're spending on groceries or making smart financial decisions.

So why is it so important for the CSET Multiple Subject Test? Well, having a solid understanding of arithmetic can really give you an edge on the exam. It's like having a secret weapon that helps you solve math problems quickly and accurately, boosting your overall performance. And who doesn't want that?

Let's start with addition, the simplest of the four operations. It's all about combining numbers to find their total sum. We use addition in so many situations, from adding up bills to managing our budgets. In this section, we're going to dive deep into various strategies and techniques that will sharpen your addition skills. With these tricks up your sleeve, you'll be able to do mental calculations in a flash and tackle even the trickiest addition problems with confidence.

Now, let's move on to subtraction, the opposite of addition. Subtraction is all about taking away one number from another to find the difference. It's a skill we use when we want to compare things or figure out how much is left after we take something away. We're going to make subtraction super relatable by using real-life examples and walking you through each step. By the end of this section, you'll become a subtraction superstar, ready to conquer any subtraction problem that comes your way.

Next up is multiplication, and this one is really cool. It's like taking addition to the next level. Multiplication is all about finding the total when we have equal groups or repeated numbers. It might not seem like a big deal, but multiplication is actually super important for solving problems related to rates, proportions, and scaling. We're going to show you different ways to multiply, from the traditional methods to mental math tricks and shortcuts. Once you master multiplication, you'll be able to tackle even the toughest problems like a pro.

Last but not least, we have division. This is the opposite of multiplication and it's all about splitting things into equal parts. We use division when we want to share something among a group, figure out rates or prices, or work with fractions or ratios. Division might seem a bit intimidating at first, but don't worry, we've got your back. We'll uncover all the division strategies, tips, and tricks, so you'll be able to handle any division problem that comes your way with ease.

So get ready, because we're about to embark on an exciting journey through the world of arithmetic and basic operations. Think of it as a quest to uncover the hidden beauty and power of numbers. This book is going to be your trusty guide as we navigate through these concepts and turn you into a confident math whiz. At Test Treasure Publication, we're not just here to teach you how to solve problems, we want to inspire you, to help you reach your full potential, and make math an extraordinary experience. So come on, let's unlock the infinite possibilities that await us in the world of arithmetic and basic operations. Together, we're unstoppable!

Algebraic Concepts

You know, when I hear the term "algebraic concepts," my mind starts to wander. It makes me think about the intricate relationships between variables and the patterns that unfold from those relationships. It's like being able to dissect and solve all sorts of equations and inequalities, from the simple ones to the mind-bogglingly complex. Algebra is this magical tool that helps us make sense of abstract ideas and connect them to real-life situations.

But let's talk about why algebraic concepts are such a big deal, especially when it comes to the CSET Multiple Subject Test. I'm telling you, this math subtest will throw all kinds of questions your way that require a deep understanding of algebraic operations, equations, and functions. And trust me, mastering these concepts will do wonders for your problem-solving skills. It's like unlocking this secret power that allows you to approach even the trickiest math problems with confidence.

Now, here's the thing about algebraic concepts – they're not just confined to math. Nope, they're everywhere, creeping into other fields like science, economics, and engineering. Heck, you'll even find them in your everyday life. They're like the hidden force behind calculating population growth, analyzing data trends, or figuring out the best way to price something. Algebra is the secret sauce that makes all these calculations possible.

But here's the juicy bit: to really get a grip on algebraic concepts, you need to be open-minded and ready to see things from different angles. Approach it with a growth mindset, ya know? And that's why we, at Test Treasure Publication, are all about sparking your curiosity and encouraging you to dive deep into the world of algebra. Our study materials are carefully crafted to ignite that flame inside you, pushing you to explore this fascinating subject.

In this journey of ours, we'll tackle all sorts of algebraic marvels. We'll start from the basics, covering things like variables and expressions, building up to the nitty-gritty of linear and quadratic equations. And hey, don't you worry! We'll be right there with you as we unravel the complexities of graphing and interpreting functions. By the time we're done, you'll have a rock-solid understanding of how graphs and equations dance together.

But it doesn't stop there. Brace yourself for the mind-blowing world of mathematical modeling. This is where algebra takes on a practical dimension. We'll teach you how to take real-world situations and turn them into mathematical equations. And trust me, when you start analyzing the patterns that emerge, you'll feel like you're solving puzzles, one step at a time. It's like a systematic and logical approach to problem-solving.

So, my friend, get ready to embrace your inner math geek and let us be your guiding light in this adventure. Our study guides, interactive flashcards, and online materials are all designed to be your compass as you navigate the vast landscape of algebraic knowledge. Together, we'll unlock the secrets of equations, tap into the potential of variables, and embark on a journey that will leave you enlightened, both academically and professionally.

Come join us at Test Treasure Publication, where we're all about going above and beyond. This is not your ordinary learning experience, my friend. With our support, you'll not only conquer the CSET Multiple Subject Test but also develop a lifelong love for algebraic concepts. And mark my words, that love will open endless doors of opportunities in your academic and professional pursuits.

Geometry and Measurement

In this vast world of Geometry, we're about to go on a crazy adventure through lines, angles, and all kinds of crazy shapes. Brace yourself for the mind-blowing world of symmetry and transformation, where shapes do tricks like reflecting and rotating. It's like a magic show, but with shapes! And let me tell you, circles are the stars of the show. These dudes have the smoothest curves and there's this thing called pi that's been driving mathematicians nuts for ages.

But that's not all! We're also gonna dive into the secrets hidden in triangles and complex polyhedra. We're gonna uncover the mysteries of congruence, similarity, and proportionality. It's all about finding balance and beauty in these geometric forms. And just when you thought things couldn't get any crazier, we're gonna tackle solid geometry. Prepare yourself for a three-dimensional wonderland of prisms, pyramids, and all sorts of crazy shapes that'll blow your mind.

But hold your horses, 'cause Geometry ain't the whole story here. We're gonna team up with Measurement to bring our mathematical world to life. It's all about quantifying and making sense of the world around us. Measurement lets us conquer uncertainty and gives us a way to be objective in this ever-changing universe.

And guess what? Arithmetic and Geometry are like best buds. We're gonna explore different units, both standard and wacky. We'll travel miles to kilometers, inches to centimeters, gallons to liters - you name it, we'll convert it. We're gonna dig deep into the world of area, figuring out how to measure those two-dimensional shapes and what makes 'em tick.

But we're not stopping there! We're gonna venture beyond two dimensions and dive into volume and capacity. We'll explore the depths of solids, calculating how much they can hold. Measurements can be confusing, but we're gonna crack the code and figure out the relationships between length, area, volume, and all those fancy units.

At Test Treasure Publication, we're gonna make all this crazy stuff super easy to understand. We believe that learning Geometry and Measurement isn't just about checking off a task, it's about unraveling the mysteries of our world. It's about discovering the harmony that's hidden within the numbers and shapes around us.

So let's go on this epic journey together. Test Treasure Publication is gonna give you the tools and confidence you need to conquer the CSET Multiple Subject Test. We've crafted study materials that'll inspire you, fill you with knowledge, and guide you to success. Join us now, and get ready to see the wonders of Geometry and Measurement unfold before your very eyes. We're gonna pave the way to extraordinary success, one step at a time.

Statistics and Probability

Welcome to this exciting chapter where we will dive headfirst into the fascinating world of statistics and probability. Get ready to uncover the secrets behind data analysis and prediction as we explore the intricate relationship between these two fields.

Let's kick things off by embracing the beauty of numbers and examining the foundations of statistics. We'll start by learning how to collect and organize data, and then we'll dive deep into measures of central tendency and variability. Trust me, these tools will help you unravel the hidden secrets concealed within datasets.

But we're not going to stop there, folks. We're going to bring those numbers to life with graphical representations. Imagine bar graphs, histograms, and scatterplots that illuminate the distribution and characteristics of data. These visual aids will give you a whole new understanding of how data can be communicated and interpreted effectively.

Next up, get ready to delve into the realm of inferential statistics. This is where we turn data into knowledge, my friends. We'll teach you the art of making predictions and drawing conclusions from a sample population. And how do we do it? Through hypothesis testing and confidence intervals. These skills will help you navigate uncertainty and extract meaning from limited information. By the time we're done, you'll hold the key to unlocking hidden truths within massive amounts of data.

Now, let's talk about probability. It's like the language of uncertainty, and we're about to become fluent. We'll unravel its intricacies and show you how important it is in decision-making and prediction. You'll learn how to quantify the likelihood of outcomes, from simple probability calculations to complex scenarios with multiple events. And let me tell you, the power of permutation and combination will blow your mind as you navigate through all the possibilities and probabilities.

But here's the best part, folks. We're not just going to keep this knowledge in a classroom. Oh no, we're going to apply statistics and probability to real-life situations. We'll analyze trends, make informed predictions, evaluate risks, and make crucial decisions. We'll show you examples across various industries and fields, proving the ubiquity of statistics and probability in our everyday lives. From economics to healthcare, from politics to sports, you'll witness these concepts in action and understand how they shape the world around us.

Now, it's time to put your skills to the test. We've got a comprehensive set of exercises and practice questions to challenge you. Solving word problems, analyzing data sets – these thought-provoking questions will sharpen your skills and solidify your understanding. Practice truly makes perfect, my friends.

Lastly, in this final chapter, we're giving you the strategies and tips you need to succeed. Our experienced educators and statisticians are here to guide you through the exam maze. From effective study techniques to time management strategies, we've got your back. Embrace their wisdom, embrace your potential, and get ready to unlock the doors to extraordinary success.

So, come join us on this enlightening journey through statistics and probability. Embrace the power of numbers, decipher the language of uncertainty, and unlock the hidden secrets within data. At Test Treasure Publication, we believe that with the right guidance and a passion for learning, you have the power to go beyond ordinary and embark on an extraordinary path to success. Let's do this!

SECTION 4: SCIENCE

Life Sciences

Chapter 1: The Building Blocks of Life

Okay, folks, buckle up because we're about to take a wild ride into the mysterious and awe-inspiring world of life itself. In this first chapter, we're peeling back the layers and diving deep into the fundamental concepts of biology. We're talking cells, people. And not just any cells, but the incredible, mind-boggling kind that make up all living things. Get ready to have your mind blown with vibrant illustrations and straightforward explanations that will light up your brain like a firework.

We'll be shining a spotlight on the mind-blowing diversity of life forms on this planet. I'm talking everything from teeny-tiny microorganisms to mind-blowingly complex ecosystems. It's like a massive tapestry of life, interwoven and interconnected in ways you never even imagined. Trust me, you'll come out of this chapter with a newfound appreciation for the intricate and absolutely mind-blowing web of life.

Chapter 2: Genetics and Heredity

Fasten your seatbelts, because chapter two is taking us straight into the blueprint of life: genetics. We're about to unlock the secrets hidden deep within our DNA. Brace yourself for a wild ride through the mechanisms of inheritance and the mind-blowing ways that traits get passed down from one generation to the next. Punnett squares, pedigrees, and even genetic engineering will all become your allies as you navigate the twists and turns of heredity.

Chapter 3: Evolution and Adaptation

Hold on tight, friends, because we're about to blast off into the world of evolution and adaptation. This is where the magic happens, people. We're diving headfirst into the deep waters of natural selection, the force that drives the mind-blowing diversity of life on this beautiful planet of ours. From the pioneering theories of Charles Darwin to the jaw-dropping evidence that connects every single species on Earth, you'll be taken on a journey that will make your brain do somersaults.

And that's not all. We're also going to explore how organisms adapt to their ever-changing environments. Think about it: these incredible beings have learned to thrive in the face of constant change and challenge. It's absolutely mind-blowing, my friends.

Chapter 4: Ecology and the Environment

Are you ready to venture into the world of delicate relationships and intricate balances? Because that's exactly what this chapter is all about. Get ready to dive deep into the heart of ecosystems, my friends. We'll be unraveling the intricacies of food chains, energy flow, and the environmental factors that shape biodiversity. And here's the kicker: we'll also be tackling some hard-hitting issues of conservation and sustainability. It's time to face the music – we've got some work to do if we want to coexist harmoniously with Mother Nature.

Chapter 5: Human Anatomy and Physiology

The grand finale is here, folks! Brace yourselves for an up-close and personal look at the human body. We're pulling back the curtains on the mind-boggling complex system that keeps us ticking. It's all about the skeletal and muscular systems that give us the ability to move, and the intricate web of systems that keep us alive and kicking. Prepare to be blown away by the inner workings of our nervous, circulatory, and respiratory systems. This is the stuff that makes us who we are, my friends.

Now, throughout this incredible journey into the mesmerizing world of Life Sciences, just remember that Test Treasure Publication is right there by your side. We've got your back, my friend. We've created study materials that have been crafted with meticulous care and a personalized approach to learning. So, strap yourself in and get ready to unlock the mind-blowing secrets of Life Sciences as you prepare to conquer the CSET Multiple Subject Test. You've got this!

Earth and Space Sciences

Step 1: Understanding Earth's Layers

Okay, so picture this: Earth is like a mind-blowing novel, and to really get what it's all about, we gotta unwrap its layers like peeling back pages. First up, we got the crust, the tough-as-nails outer shell that keeps life going. Dive a little deeper, and you'll run into the mantle, a wild layer of molten rock and semi-solid stuff that's always on the move. And finally, at the core, there's this intense, iron-rich ball of fire, pulsing with crazy heat and pressure. It's like the heart of the whole planet, man.

Step 2: Unraveling Plate Tectonics

Alright, now that we've got the low-down on Earth's makeup, brace yourself for the rollercoaster ride of plate tectonics. Picture a puzzle, with these different chunks of land and ocean fitting together and sliding around like they've got a mind of their own. That slow-but-steady movement isn't just for show, though—it shapes our continents, builds mountains, and sets off earthquakes and volcanoes. And there are all these types of plate boundaries, where stuff crashes together or pulls apart. It's wild, man—the power beneath our feet is something else.

Step 3: Peering into the Stars

Now, I want you to look up, way up, and let your mind explode with the stars that paint the night sky. There's a whole big universe out there to explore, from the planets in our solar system to the moons that orbit them. And don't forget about the other crazy stuff happening out there. In Earth and Space Sciences, we're gonna be like astronauts, taking a deep dive into our solar system and beyond, learning about all these mind-blowing wonders and cosmic mysteries.

Step 4: The Magnificence of the Universe

But hold onto your hats, 'cause we're not stopping at our solar system. Buckle up for a trip through the mind-boggling vastness of the universe. We're gonna witness the birth of stars, exploding nebulae, and supernovae going out with a bang. Wrap your brain around light-years, those crazy units that measure how far light can travel in a whole year. And get ready to be blown away by galaxies and clusters, these architectural masterpieces that hold billions of stars and secrets we can't even fathom.

Step 5: Earth's Place in the Universe

Alright, guys, here's the final word: Earth is like a tiny player in this massive cosmic dance. We gotta step back and really think about our place in the universe. How did life even start on this little blue planet of ours? And what can we do to protect it from any cosmic threats? These big questions keep us searching for answers and push us to expand our knowledge. Let's explore this whole universe together, my friends, and let it inspire us to keep wondering and dreaming. We're starting this awe-inspiring journey, and the universe is calling our names. So let's get going and make some cosmic discoveries!

Physical Sciences

Alright, buckle up folks because we're about to embark on an epic journey through the incredible world of Physical Sciences. Get ready to explore the mysteries of matter and energy as we unravel the secrets of the universe. We're going to dive deep into the atomic and molecular structures that make up everything around us, unlocking the enigmatic dance of electrons and uncovering the wonders of chemical reactions.

But wait, there's more! We're not stopping there. We'll also venture into the wild realms of motion and forces. Newton's laws of physics will be our trusty guide as we discover the principles of work and energy. It's all about understanding how objects interact and transform in the physical world, from tiny microscopic particles to massive celestial bodies. It's mind-blowing stuff!

And get this, we're setting sail into the boundless wonders of electricity, magnetism, and optics. Get ready to wrap your head around electric circuits and all that jazz, mastering the flow of currents and the principles of resistance, voltage, and capacitance. Plus, we'll dive into the mesmerizing world of magnetism where invisible forces shape the foundations of technology. And prepare to be dazzled by the captivating phenomena of reflection, refraction, and color as we unravel the secrets of waves and particles. It's like magic, but even better because it's real!

But hold on tight because we're not done yet! We're about to venture into the mysterious realms of thermodynamics and fluid mechanics. Picture this - we're going to bring life to concepts like heat transfer and entropy, understanding how energy flows and transforms in different systems. And get this, we'll also be exploring the mind-blowing world of fluid dynamics. We're talking about the behavior of liquids and gases, from peaceful rivers to the stunning power of hurricanes. It's seriously fascinating stuff!

Throughout this wild adventure, we don't want you to just passively absorb the information. No, no, my friend. We want you to truly engage with it. Let your curiosity run wild, ask questions, and really connect with the materials on a personal level. This isn't just about learning facts; it's about fueling your thirst for knowledge and becoming a critical thinker.

And let me tell you, the knowledge you gain here is more than just a commodity. It's a treasure, my friend. It's the key to unlocking a world of possibilities. Not only will you gain a deep understanding of the natural world, but you'll also develop analytical thinking, problem-solving skills, and perseverance. You'll become a true explorer of the physical realm!

So, get ready for the ride of your life. Armed with the knowledge and skills you'll gain from this journey, you'll be prepared to tackle the challenges of the CSET Multiple Subject Test and beyond. This is your opportunity to embrace your inner scientist and embark on a thrilling odyssey of discovery. Welcome, fellow adventurer, to the captivating world of Physical Sciences. Let's do this!

Section 5: Physical Education and Human Development

Physical Education and Wellness

Alright, folks, let's get real here. We're diving headfirst into the important world of physical education and wellness. This is no ordinary subject – it's a game-changer in today's society. We're going to explore how getting off our butts and moving not only boosts our physical health, but also kicks our cognitive function into high gear. Oh, and did I mention it does wonders for our emotional well-being too? Trust me, this is some good stuff.

Now, hold on to your hats because things are about to get even more interesting. We're going to break down the key concepts and principles behind physical education and wellness. We're talking about the nitty-gritty here – the ins and outs of human anatomy and physiology. Plus, we're going to learn about the principles of exercise and fitness, and how our lifestyle choices can impact our health. Buckle up, people, it's gonna be a wild ride.

But hold up, we can't just stop there. As future educators, knowledge isn't the only thing we need. We've gotta have some kick-ass teaching strategies in our back pockets. Don't worry, we've got your back. We're going to explore all kinds of instructional approaches and techniques that will get your students pumped up and ready to go. From using technology to cater to different learning styles, we're gonna make sure you're prepared for anything that comes your way.

Now, it's time to face some hard truths. We're going to take a deep dive into the current health and wellness issues that our students are facing today. We're talking about sedentary lifestyles, junk food addictions, and the heavy weight of mental health concerns. This is some heavy stuff, guys, and we need to be prepared to tackle it head-on. It's not gonna be easy, but if we want to make a difference, we've got to be in the know.

Finally, we're gonna put all this knowledge into action. It's time to get our hands dirty and apply what we've learned. We've got all kinds of practical activities, lesson plans, and project ideas that'll have your students on their feet and begging for more. This is where ordinary teaching transforms into something extraordinary. So get ready to make a positive impact on your students' lives.

At Test Treasure Publication, we're not just here to help you pass a test. We want to empower you to become the best darn educator you can be. We want you to believe in the power of physical education and wellness. With our comprehensive study guide, we're unlocking your potential so you can create a future bursting with opportunities to make a real difference. So, join us on this journey – because when knowledge becomes exceptionalism, and ordinary teaching becomes extraordinary, we know we've done our job right.

Human Development and Psychology

Welcome, my fellow explorers, to a thrilling journey into the mysteries of human development. Buckle up as we embark on an adventure through the different stages that shape our lives, from the tiniest infants to fully-grown adults. Get ready to dive deep into the web of cognitive, physical, emotional, and social growth, uncovering the countless factors that mold our personalities and identities.

Picture this: our study materials are like bright beacons guiding us through the labyrinth of psychological theories and ideologies. No more head-scratching over enigmatic puzzles! Our resources turn complexity into clarity, making these concepts accessible and comprehensible.

Let's kick things off with a panoramic view of developmental psychology, where we'll encounter a tapestry of key theories and frameworks that have revolutionized our understanding of human growth. Say hello to Sigmund Freud's psychosexual stages and Erik Erikson's psychosocial theory, among others. It's like stepping into a wonderland of perspectives that showcase how multifaceted our development truly is.

But wait, the adventure doesn't stop there! Our next destination is the captivating world of infancy and childhood, where the transformative process of life's first steps begins. We'll dive headfirst into the mysterious realm of attachment, discovering just how crucial secure relationships are in shaping our personalities and emotional well-being.

Fasten your seatbelts again as we move on to adolescence, a stage bursting with self-discovery and identity formation. Peer influence, cognitive development, and the emergence of moral reasoning will take center stage, giving you the tools to navigate this rollercoaster period with confidence and grace.

Now, let's flip the narrative to adulthood. Brace yourself for a profound expedition into the complex world of maturity, where the physical, psychological, and social aspects of adulthood come together in a symphony of experiences. Love and intimacy will be under our microscope, as we unravel the intricate dynamics of romantic relationships.

With the help of our study materials, you'll embark on a journey of self-reflection and personal growth. We're committed to your success, empowering you with the knowledge and understanding of the human psyche. Get ready to foster empathy, resilience, and a deep appreciation for the diverse tapestry of human experience.

At Test Treasure Publication, we invite you to join the quest for enlightenment. Let the intricacies of human development and psychology become a source of fascination, discovery, and self-discovery. Together, we'll illuminate the path to extraordinary success. Embrace the transformative power of knowledge and let's unlock the secrets of the human mind, uncovering the infinite possibilities that lie within each and every one of us.

Section 6: Visual and Performing Arts

Visual Arts

As we crack open the pages of our trusty study guide, we embark on a thrilling voyage. It's not just about strokes of a paintbrush or sculptures molded from clay. No, it's about unearthing the fascinating stories behind each masterpiece, digging deep to unravel the secrets held within. From the intricacies of Renaissance art to the audaciousness of modern abstract expressionism, we're here to take you on an immersive journey through time, showcasing the wondrous evolution of artistic expression.

See, we get it. Visual Arts isn't just about cramming in facts and dates. It's a language that speaks straight to your soul, a form of communication that goes beyond mere words. With that in mind, our study materials go above and beyond to capture the very essence of each artistic movement. They allow you to truly grasp the motivations and emotions that fueled these brilliant artists as they created their celebrated works.

Picture this: you stepping into the studio of the great Impressionists, witnessing firsthand the magical play of light and color that brought their enchanting landscapes to life. Imagine feeling the raw passion and intense emotions of the Expressionists as they poured their heart and soul onto their canvases. And let's not forget the realm of sculpture, where bronze and marble seem to come alive in the hands of geniuses like Michelangelo and Rodin. Our study guide is a portal into these breathtaking worlds, giving you the chance to experience art like never before.

But we're not done yet. See, our dedication to Visual Arts goes way beyond what's written in your textbook. We also offer a set of flashy flashcards that don't just reinforce your knowledge of key terms and concepts; they also showcase the mind-blowing diversity of artistic styles out there. From the delicate lines of pen and ink illustrations to the bold and revolutionary strokes of abstract expressionism, these flashcards give you the chance to truly appreciate the uniqueness of each art form.

But hold your horses, there's more! On top of all that, Test Treasure Publication also provides an unforgettable online study platform. Picture yourself exploring virtual galleries filled with the world's greatest artworks. You can zoom in close to examine every intricate detail and even engage with interactive quizzes that test your art history know-how. We've created an environment of active learning, where you can truly immerse yourself in the material and make it your own.

At Test Treasure Publication, we firmly believe that Visual Arts isn't just some academic subject to tick off your list. No, it's a gateway to personal growth and self-expression. We encourage you to unleash your own creative potential, to experiment with various art mediums, and to nurture your unique artistic voice. Our study materials act as the catalyst for your own artistic journey, igniting a passion for art that will stick with you long after the exam is over.

In the realm of Visual Arts, Test Treasure Publication is more than just a stuffy study guide. We're your trusted mentor, your loyal companion on this breathtaking artistic adventure. So, why not join us on this extraordinary odyssey? Together, let's unlock the secrets of the canvas and embark on a journey that transcends the mundane. Let's delve into the power of art to captivate, inspire, and transform.

Music and Performing Arts

Let's dive into the wonderland of music theory, my friends. Get ready to explore the language that speaks to every soul, breaking down boundaries and melting hearts. We'll unravel the secrets behind rhythm, melody, harmony, and structure - the foundations that make our favorite songs come alive. Our mission is to light a fire in your belly, stirring up a passion for music that will set your creativity ablaze.

But hold onto your hats, because we won't stop at theory alone. Oh no, my friends, we believe that true musicianship blooms through practice and performance. So get ready to dive headfirst into a treasure trove of techniques, exercises, and songs for every instrument and every singing voice. It's time to sharpen those skills, my friends, and bring music to life with every note and every breath.

But wait, there's more! We know that the stage has a magnetic pull, beckoning artists to bask in its spotlight. In the mystical realm of the performing arts, we'll reveal the tricks that'll turn you into a captivating performer. We'll guide you through acting techniques, helping you unleash your inner star. And we'll shape your stage presence, so you can command the room and leave your audience in awe. Trust us, my friends, we'll be your loyal sidekick on this whimsical journey, giving you the courage to take center stage and shine your brightest.

Yet, here's the cool part: It goes beyond just techniques and fancy moves. When it comes to music and the performing arts, my friends, we're talking about something profound. Something that can stir your spirit, move your soul, and build connections where none existed before. So join us, won't you? Let's dive into deep conversations, exploring the power that music and performing arts have to touch lives and transcend cultures. We'll open your eyes to the boundless potential of this enchanting world.

In this quest, my friends, we're building a family. A tribe of passionate musicians and performers, brought together by a shared love for the arts. Our online forums and study groups aren't just a place to learn - they're a hub for collaboration and inspiration. So come, connect with kindred spirits, and let the magic of music and the performing arts carry us all forward.

Can I share a little secret with you? This journey isn't just about getting a fancy diploma or a shiny medal. No, my friends, it's about embracing the wonder of it all. Music and the performing arts aren't boring subjects we cram into our brains. They're passions that bloom and grow with us throughout our lives. So let's shake things up, my friends. Let's explore new genres, dance to different beats, and let our imagination run wild. Let's make our hearts sing like never before.

At Test Treasure Publication, we've got you covered. We're your trusted guide, armed with tools, resources, and unwavering support. We're here to turn your dreams in music and the performing arts into reality. So take our hand, my friends, and let's embark on this extraordinary journey together. With our guidance, you'll find your rhythm, reach for the stars, and discover the truly transformative power of music and the performing arts.

7.1 FULL-LENGTH PRACTICE TEST 1

Reading, Language, and Literature:

Question 1: Which literary device is used when words are intentionally given human traits?

A) Irony

B) Alliteration

C) Personification

D) Metaphor

Question 2: The main idea of a text can usually be found in the:

A) Conclusion

B) Body

C) Introduction

D) Title

Question 3: Which of the following is NOT a vowel sound?

A) A

B) E

C) X

D) O

Question 4: In which point of view is the narrator not a character in the story?

A) First Person

B) Second Person

C) Third Person Limited

D) Third Person Omniscient

Question 5: What does an adverb typically modify?

A) Noun

B) Adjective

C) Verb

D) Pronoun

History and Social Science:

Question 6: What is the main function of the U.S. legislative branch?

A) Interpret laws

B) Enforce laws

C) Make laws

D) Review laws

Question 7: During which war was the Treaty of Versailles signed?

A) Revolutionary War

B) World War I

C) World War II

D) Korean War

Question 8: What economic system is characterized by private ownership of goods and free market?

A) Socialism

B) Capitalism

C) Feudalism

D) Communism

Question 9: Who was the first President of the United States?

A) Thomas Jefferson

B) George Washington

C) Abraham Lincoln

D) Benjamin Franklin

Question 10: The Emancipation Proclamation freed slaves in which areas?

A) All of the United States

B) The Union States

C) The Confederate States

D) The Border States

Mathematics:

Question 11: If $y=3x+5$, what is the value of y when $x=2$?

A) 9

B) 10

C) 11

D) 14

Question 12: What is the next number in the sequence 2, 6, 12, 20, ...?

A) 30

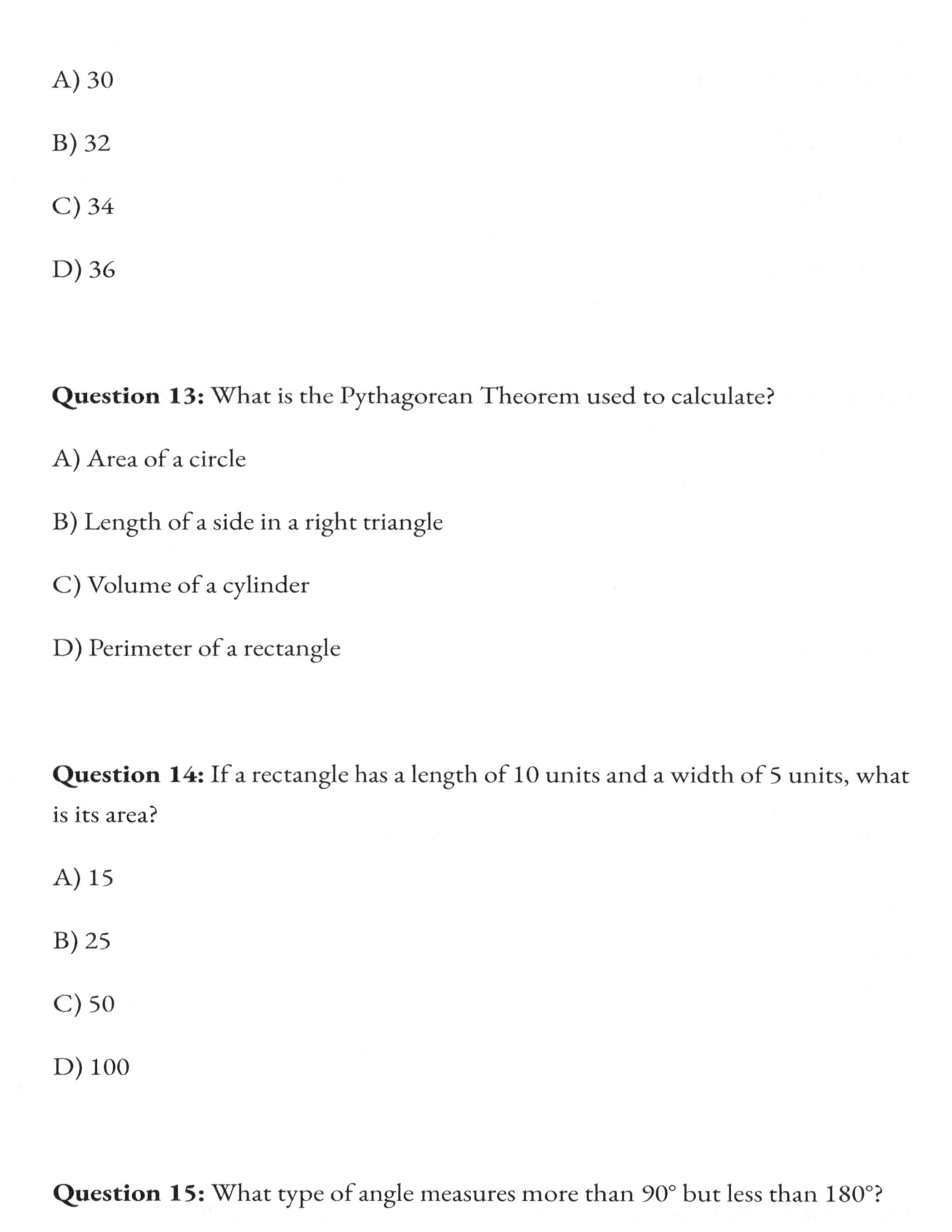

B) 32

C) 34

D) 36

Question 13: What is the Pythagorean Theorem used to calculate?

A) Area of a circle

B) Length of a side in a right triangle

C) Volume of a cylinder

D) Perimeter of a rectangle

Question 14: If a rectangle has a length of 10 units and a width of 5 units, what is its area?

A) 15

B) 25

C) 50

D) 100

Question 15: What type of angle measures more than 90° but less than 180°?

A) Acute angle

B) Obtuse angle

C) Right angle

D) Straight angle

Science:

Question 16: What is the process by which plants make their own food using sunlight?

A) Respiration

B) Fermentation

C) Photosynthesis

D) Digestion

Question 17: Which planet in our solar system is known as the Red Planet?

A) Venus

B) Mars

C) Jupiter

D) Saturn

Question 18: What is the atomic number of carbon?

A) 4

B) 6

C) 8

D) 12

Question 19: In which layer of Earth's atmosphere do most weather events occur?

A) Stratosphere

B) Troposphere

C) Mesosphere

D) Thermosphere

Question 20: What is the main gas found in the Earth's atmosphere?

A) Oxygen

B) Carbon Dioxide

C) Hydrogen

D) Nitrogen

Physical Education and Human Development:

Question 21: Which nutrient is primarily used by the body for energy?

A) Proteins

B) Carbohydrates

C) Vitamins

D) Minerals

Question 22: What is the recommended amount of physical activity for adults per week according to the U.S. Department of Health and Human Services?

A) 75 minutes of vigorous-intensity exercise

B) 150 minutes of moderate-intensity exercise

C) 200 minutes of light-intensity exercise

D) Both A and B

Question 23: Which bone protects the brain?

A) Femur

B) Skull

C) Ribcage

D) Spine

Question 24: In which developmental stage does puberty typically occur?

A) Infancy

B) Early Childhood

C) Adolescence

D) Adulthood

Question 25: What is the primary focus of motor development during the first year of life?

A) Coordination

B) Strength

C) Flexibility

D) Balance

Reading, Language, and Literature:

Question 26: What term refers to the repetition of consonant sounds at the beginning of words?

A) Onomatopoeia

B) Metaphor

C) Alliteration

D) Hyperbole

Question 27: What is the main purpose of a persuasive text?

A) To entertain

B) To inform

C) To persuade

D) To narrate

Question 28: What type of conflict is man vs. nature?

A) Internal Conflict

B) External Conflict

C) Societal Conflict

D) Interpersonal Conflict

Question 29: In a play, what term refers to the notes provided to explain how a character should move or speak?

A) Dialogue

B) Stage Directions

C) Monologue

D) Acts

Question 30: What is a synonym for "benevolent"?

A) Malicious

B) Kind

C) Hostile

D) Lazy

History and Social Science:

Question 31: What was the main goal of the Civil Rights Movement in the United States?

A) Economic Prosperity

B) Equal Rights for all Races

C) Military Supremacy

D) Industrialization

Question 32: Who wrote the Declaration of Independence?

A) James Madison

B) Benjamin Franklin

C) Thomas Jefferson

D) John Adams

Question 33: What is the study of the production, distribution, and consumption of goods and services?

A) Sociology

B) Anthropology

C) Economics

D) Geography

Question 34: During what war did trench warfare become common?

A) American Civil War

B) World War I

C) World War II

D) Vietnam War

Question 35: What year did the United States officially become independent?

A) 1776

B) 1783

C) 1791

D) 1800

Mathematics:

Question 36: What is the solution to the equation $2x-4=10$?

A) x = 3

B) x = 7

C) x = 5

D) x = 1

Question 37: A triangle has angles of 40°, 60°, and what other angle?

A) 40°

B) 60°

C) 80°

D) 100°

Question 38: What is the volume of a cube with sides of length 3 cm?

A) 9 cm³

B) 27 cm³

C) 36 cm³

D) 81 cm³

Question 39: Which term refers to the steepness of a line on a graph?

A) Y-Intercept

B) X-Intercept

C) Slope

D) Origin

Question 40: If a spinner is divided into 5 equal parts and you spin it once, what is the probability of landing on one specific section?

A) 1/2

B) 1/3

C) 1/5

D) 2/5

Science:

Question 41: During which process do plants release oxygen and convert stored energy into usable forms for growth and metabolism?

A) Transpiration

B) Germination

C) Respiration

D) Absorption

Question 42: Which element has the atomic number 22?

A) Titanium (Ti)

B) Chromium (Cr)

C) Vanadium (V)

D) Manganese (Mn)

Question 43: Which planet is the largest in our solar system and is often called the "Gas Giant"?

A) Jupiter

B) Saturn

C) Neptune

D) Uranus

Question 44: What type of organism is a fungus?

A) Plant

B) Animal

C) Bacteria

D) Neither plant nor animal

Question 45: What is the primary function of ozone (O3) in the Earth's atmosphere?

A) Absorbing ultraviolet (UV) radiation

B) Facilitating combustion reactions

C) Supporting plant respiration

D) Contributing to the greenhouse effect

Physical Education and Human Development:

Question 46: Which vitamin is synthesized in the skin in response to sunlight?

A) Vitamin A

B) Vitamin B

C) Vitamin C

D) Vitamin D

Question 47: What is the term for the natural, physical decline that's associated with aging?

A) Atrophy

B) Senescence

C) Metabolism

D) Catabolism

Question 48: Which part of the brain is responsible for balance and coordination?

A) Cerebrum

B) Cerebellum

C) Medulla Oblongata

D) Thalamus

Question 49: What are the smallest structural and functional units of an organism, typically microscopic?

A) Organs

B) Tissues

C) Cells

D) Systems

Question 50: What is the leading cause of death in the United States?

A) Cancer

B) Heart Disease

C) Respiratory Diseases

D) Accidents

Reading, Language, and Literature:

Question 51: What is the antonym of "arduous"?

A) Difficult

B) Easy

C) Challenging

D) Demanding

Question 52: Which literary device involves the repetition of initial consonant sounds in neighboring words or syllables?

A) Simile

B) Metaphor

C) Alliteration

D) Personification

Question 53: Which of the following is an example of a primary source?

A) A history textbook

B) A biographical film

C) An original letter from a historical figure

D) A review of a novel

Question 54: What does a semicolon typically connect?

A) Two unrelated sentences

B) Two closely related sentences

C) A question and an answer

D) A definition and an example

Question 55: Which narrative point of view uses "he," "she," or "they" to tell the story?

A) First Person

B) Second Person

C) Third Person

D) Omniscient

History and Social Science:

Question 56: Which of the following U.S. Presidents is most closely associated with the New Deal, a series of programs and reforms aimed at recovering from the Great Depression?

A) Herbert Hoover

B) Franklin D. Roosevelt

C) Woodrow Wilson

D) Harry S. Truman

Question 57: What event started the American Revolution?

A) Boston Tea Party

B) Boston Massacre

C) Signing of the Declaration of Independence

D) Battle of Lexington and Concord

Question 58: What is the primary focus of microeconomics?

A) Individual Businesses and Consumers

B) Global Economic Trends

C) National Economic Policies

D) Intercontinental Trade Regulations

Question 59: Which civilization is known for building large pyramids?

A) Greek

B) Roman

C) Chinese

D) Egyptian

Question 60: During which war was the Emancipation Proclamation issued?

A) Revolutionary War

B) Civil War

C) World War I

D) World War II

Mathematics:

Question 61: If a triangle has sides of length 3, 4, and 5, what type of triangle is it?

A) Equilateral

B) Isosceles

C) Scalene

D) Right

Question 62: What is the midpoint of the line segment with endpoints (2,4) and (6,8)?

A) (4,4)

B) (4,6)

C) (8,12)

D) (3,5)

Question 63: If $f(x)=2x+5$, what is $f(3)$?

A) 9

B) 11

C) 6

D) 8

Question 64: What is the next term in the sequence 2, 4, 8, 16, ...?

A) 18

B) 24

C) 32

D) 36

Question 65: A circle's circumference is 18π. What is the radius?

A) 3

B) 6

C) 9

D) 12

Science:

Question 66: What type of rock is formed by the cooling and solidification of lava or magma?

A) Sedimentary

B) Metamorphic

C) Igneous

D) Limestone

Question 67: Which part of the plant is responsible for photosynthesis?

A) Root

B) Stem

C) Leaf

D) Flower

Question 68: What is the chemical formula for water?

A) H_2O

B) CO_2

C) O_2

D) N_2

Question 69: Which planet is the largest in the Solar System?

A) Venus

B) Mars

C) Jupiter

D) Saturn

Question 70: What is the primary purpose of DNA?

A) Respiratory Function

B) Digestion

C) Storing Genetic Information

D) Blood Circulation

Physical Education and Human Development:

Question 71: What is the name of the muscle in the upper arm that is used to flex the elbow?

A) Gluteus Maximus

B) Hamstring

C) Bicep

D) Quadriceps

Question 72: Which of the following physical activities best promotes cardio-vascular endurance in elementary school children?

A) Sprinting

B) Jump rope

C) Weight lifting

D) Long-distance running

Question 73: What nutrient is essential for the building and repair of tissues, including muscles and organs?

A) Fats

B) Proteins

C) Fiber

D) Vitamins

Question 74: What is the main function of the skeletal system?

A) Digestion

B) Providing Structure and Support

C) Respiration

D) Circulation

Question 75: Which health-related factor can be improved by regular aerobic exercise?

A) Muscle Strength

B) Joint Flexibility

C) Cardiovascular Endurance

D) Eye-hand Coordination

Reading, Language, and Literature:

Question 76: Which poetic device repeats consonant sounds at the beginning of words?

A) Assonance

B) Alliteration

C) Onomatopoeia

D) Hyperbole

Question 77: What is the main purpose of an index in a non-fiction book?

A) To define terms

B) To summarize the book

C) To list topics and their page numbers

D) To introduce the main concepts

Question 78: What type of pronoun is used to show ownership?

A) Interrogative

B) Indefinite

C) Demonstrative

D) Possessive

Question 79: Which literary term describes a brief story used to illustrate a point?

A) Allegory

B) Anecdote

C) Satire

D) Paradox

Question 80: What is the climax of a story?

A) The resolution

B) The beginning

C) The most exciting point

D) The introduction of the conflict

History and Social Science:

Question 81: Which amendment to the U.S. Constitution abolished slavery?

A) First Amendment

B) Thirteenth Amendment

C) Fifteenth Amendment

D) Nineteenth Amendment

Question 82: Who was the first female Prime Minister of the United Kingdom?

A) Margaret Thatcher

B) Theresa May

C) Angela Merkel

D) Indira Gandhi

Question 83: During which period did the Renaissance occur?

A) 12th-14th Centuries

B) 14th-17th Centuries

C) 17th-19th Centuries

D) 19th-20th Centuries

Question 84: What does the term "Cold War" refer to?

A) A war fought in cold climates

B) A period of non-violent tension between the USA and the USSR

C) A conflict over Arctic territories

D) A series of winter military exercises

Question 85: What is the capital city of France?

A) Madrid

B) Rome

C) London

D) Paris

Mathematics:

Question 86: If $y=3x-4$, what is the value of y when $x=2$?

A) 2

B) 4

C) 6

D) 8

Question 87: What is the sum of the interior angles of a hexagon?

A) 180°

B) 540°

C) 720°

D) 900°

Question 88: What is the probability of rolling an even number on a standard six-sided die?

A) 1/2

B) 1/3

C) 1/4

D) 2/3

Question 89: If a triangle has angles of 60° and 70°, what is the measure of the third angle?

A) 30°

B) 40°

C) 50°

D) 60°

Question 90: A 15% discount is applied to an item that costs $200. What is the sale price?

A) $30

B) $170

C) $150

D) $185

Science:

Question 91: What is the term for the movement of water from the roots to the leaves of a plant, driven by factors such as evaporation **and capillary action?**

A) Osmosis

B) Translocation

C) Transpiration

D) Respiration

Question 92: Which formula represents the compound formed between sodium and chlorine?

A) $NaCl_2$

B) Na_2Cl

C) NaCl

D) Na_2Cl_3

Question 93: What phase of matter has a definite volume but no definite shape?

A) Solid

B) Liquid

C) Gas

D) Plasma

Question 94: Which vitamin is essential for blood clotting?

A) Vitamin A

B) Vitamin

B C) Vitamin C

D) Vitamin K

Question 95: What type of celestial object is the Sun?

A) Planet

B) Comet

C) Asteroid

D) Star

Physical Education and Human Development:

Question 96: Which type of exercise focuses on increasing muscle size and strength?

A) Aerobic

B) Anaerobic

C) Stretching

D) Yoga

Question 97: What is the Body Mass Index (BMI) used to assess?

A) Muscular Strength

B) Flexibility

C) Body Composition

D) Cardiovascular Fitness

Question 98: Which nutrient is responsible for regulating various physiological processes, such as nerve function and fluid balance?

A) Sodium

B) Potassium

C) Calcium

D) Magnesium

Question 99: What is a common injury that occurs from overuse or misuse of a joint?

A) Sprain

B) Bruise

C) Fracture

D) Strain

Question 100: What does the acronym "RICE" stand for in the context of treating injuries?

A) Rest, Ice, Compression, Elevation

B) Rice, Ice, Compression, Exercise

C) Rest, Ice, Compression, Exercise

D) Rice, Ice, Cold, Elevation

7.2 Answer Sheet - Practice Test 1

1. Answer: C) Personification

Explanation: Personification is the attribution of human traits or characteristics to non-human entities.

2. Answer: C) Introduction

Explanation: The main idea is often introduced in the opening paragraph or introduction of a text.

3. Answer: C) X

Explanation: X is a consonant, not a vowel.

4. Answer: D) Third Person Omniscient

Explanation: In Third Person Omniscient point of view, the narrator knows all and sees all but is not a character in the story.

5. Answer: C) Verb

Explanation: An adverb typically modifies a verb, describing how the action is performed.

6. Answer: C) Make laws

Explanation: The main function of the legislative branch, consisting of the Senate and House of Representatives, is to create laws.

7. Answer: B) World War I

Explanation: The Treaty of Versailles was signed to end World War I.

8. Answer: B) Capitalism

Explanation: Capitalism emphasizes private ownership and the free market system.

9. Answer: B) George Washington

Explanation: George Washington was the first President of the United States, serving from 1789 to 1797.

10. Answer: C) The Confederate States

Explanation: The Emancipation Proclamation specifically freed slaves in the Confederate States, not in the Union or Border States.

11. Answer: C) 11

Explanation: By substituting $x=2$ into the equation $y=3x+5$, we get $y=3 \cdot 2+5=6+5=11$.

12. Answer: A) 30

Explanation: The pattern is given by adding consecutive odd numbers to the previous term. So, the next number is $20+10=30$.

13. Answer: B) Length of a side in a right triangle

Explanation: The Pythagorean Theorem is used to find the length of a side in a right triangle, using the formula $a^2+b^2=c^2$, where c is the hypotenuse.

14. Answer: C) 50

Explanation: The area of a rectangle is given by the formula length×width, so the area is 10×5=50 square units.

15. Answer: B) Obtuse angle

Explanation: An obtuse angle measures more than 90° but less than 180°.

16. Answer: C) Photosynthesis

Explanation: Photosynthesis is the process by which green plants use sunlight to synthesize foods from carbon dioxide and water.

17. Answer: B) Mars

Explanation: Mars is often referred to as the Red Planet because of its reddish appearance.

18. Answer: B) 6

Explanation: The atomic number of carbon is 6, which means it has 6 protons in its nucleus.

19. Answer: B) Troposphere

Explanation: Most weather phenomena occur in the troposphere, the lowest layer of Earth's atmosphere.

20. Answer: D) Nitrogen

Explanation: Nitrogen makes up about 78% of Earth's atmosphere, making it the most prevalent gas.

21. Answer: B) Carbohydrates

Explanation: Carbohydrates are the body's primary source of energy.

22. Answer: D) Both A and B

Explanation: The U.S. Department of Health and Human Services recommends either 150 minutes of moderate-intensity or 75 minutes of vigorous-intensity exercise per week for adults.

23. Answer: B) Skull

Explanation: The skull is the bone structure that encases and protects the brain.

24. Answer: C) Adolescence

Explanation: Puberty typically occurs during adolescence, which is the transitional phase from childhood to adulthood.

25. Answer: A) Coordination

Explanation: During the first year of life, the primary focus of motor development is the development of coordination, allowing infants to control and integrate their movements.

26. Answer: C) Alliteration

Explanation: Alliteration refers to the repetition of consonant sounds at the beginning of words in close proximity.

27. Answer: C) To persuade

Explanation: The main purpose of persuasive text is to convince the reader of a particular viewpoint or action.

28. Answer: B) External Conflict

Explanation: Man vs. nature represents an external conflict, where the protagonist faces challenges from natural forces.

29. Answer: B) Stage Directions

Explanation: Stage directions are instructions in the script of a play that indicate movement, position, or tone of an actor, or the sound effects and lighting.

30. Answer: B) Kind

Explanation: "Benevolent" means well-meaning and kind, so the synonym is "kind."

31. Answer: B) Equal Rights for all Races

Explanation: The Civil Rights Movement in the United States sought to end racial segregation and discrimination and achieve equal rights for all races.

32. Answer: C) Thomas Jefferson

Explanation: Thomas Jefferson was the principal author of the Declaration of Independence.

33. Answer: C) Economics

Explanation: Economics is the study of how societies, governments, businesses, households, and individuals produce, distribute, and consume goods and services.

34. Answer: B) World War I

Explanation: Trench warfare was a common military tactic during World War I.

35. Answer: B) 1783

Explanation: Although the Declaration of Independence was adopted on July 4, 1776, the United States officially became independent in 1783 with the signing of the Treaty of Paris.

36. Answer: B) x = 7

Explanation: To solve the equation, you can add 4 to both sides, getting $2x=14$, and then divide by 2 to find $x=7$.

37. Answer: C) 80°

Explanation: The angles of a triangle sum to 180°, so the third angle is 180−40−60=80 degrees.

38. Answer: B) 27 cm³

Explanation: The volume of a cube is given by s^3, where s is the side length. So, the volume is 3^3=27 cubic centimeters.

39. Answer: C) Slope

Explanation: The slope of a line refers to its steepness and is often represented by the letter *m*.

40. Answer: C) 1/5

Explanation: Since the spinner is divided into 5 equal parts, the probability of landing on one specific section is 1/5.

41. Answer: C) Respiration

Explanation: Respiration is the process in which plants release oxygen and convert stored energy into usable forms for growth and metabolism.

42. Answer: A) Titanium (Ti)

Explanation: Titanium has the atomic number 22.

43. Answer: A) Jupiter

Explanation: Jupiter is the largest planet in our solar system and is commonly referred to as the "Gas Giant."

44. Answer: D) Neither plant nor animal

Explanation: Fungi are distinct from plants and animals and have their own kingdom. They share characteristics with both but are classified separately.

45. Answer: A) Absorbing ultraviolet (UV) radiation

Explanation: Ozone in the stratosphere absorbs and protects the Earth from harmful ultraviolet (UV) radiation.

46. Answer: D) Vitamin D

Explanation: Vitamin D is synthesized in the skin in response to sunlight.

47. Answer: B) Senescence

Explanation: Senescence refers to the biological aging process, involving the gradual deterioration of function characteristic of most complex life forms.

48. Answer: B) Cerebellum

Explanation: The cerebellum is responsible for balance, coordination, and the timing of muscle movements.

49. Answer: C) Cells

Explanation: Cells are the smallest structural and functional units of an organism.

50. Answer: B) Heart Disease

Explanation: As of the current statistics, heart disease is the leading cause of death in the United States.

51. Answer: B) Easy

Explanation: "Arduous" means requiring a lot of effort, so the antonym is "easy."

52. Answer: C) Alliteration

Explanation: Alliteration involves the repetition of initial consonant sounds.

53. Answer: C) An original letter from a historical figure

Explanation: A primary source is a document or physical object created during the time under study, such as an original letter from a historical figure.

54. Answer: B) Two closely related sentences

Explanation: A semicolon is used to link two closely related independent clauses.

55. Answer: C) Third Person

Explanation: In the third-person point of view, the narrator uses "he," "she," or "they" to tell the story.

56. Answer: B) Franklin D. Roosevelt

Explanation: Franklin D. Roosevelt is best known for implementing the New Deal, a series of federal programs, public work projects, and financial reforms aimed at helping the U.S. recover from the Great Depression in the 1930s.

57. Answer: D) Battle of Lexington and Concord

Explanation: The Battle of Lexington and Concord, fought on April 19, 1775, marked the beginning of the American Revolutionary War.

58. Answer: A) Individual Businesses and Consumers

Explanation: Microeconomics studies the behavior of individual businesses and consumers and how they make decisions.

59. Answer: D) Egyptian

Explanation: The ancient Egyptians are famous for building large pyramids, particularly as tombs for their pharaohs.

60. Answer: B) Civil War

Explanation: The Emancipation Proclamation was issued during the American Civil War.

61. Answer: D) Right

Explanation: A triangle with sides of length 3, 4, and 5 is a right triangle, as it follows the Pythagorean Theorem $3^2+4^2=5^2$.

62. Answer: B) (4,6)

Explanation: The midpoint is found by averaging the x-values and y-values of the endpoints: $(2+6/2, 4+8/2)=(4,6)$.

63. Answer: B) 11

Explanation: To find $f(3)$, simply substitute $x=3$ into the equation: $f(3)=2(3)+5=6+5=11$.

64. Answer: C) 32

Explanation: The sequence is doubling each term, so the next term is 32.

65. Answer: C) 9

Explanation: Using the formula for the circumference of a circle $C=2\pi r$, we can find the radius: $18\pi=2\pi r \Rightarrow r=9$.

66. Answer: C) Igneous

Explanation: Igneous rocks are formed by the cooling and solidification of lava or magma.

67. Answer: C) Leaf

Explanation: The leaves of the plant contain chloroplasts, which are the main sites of photosynthesis.

68. Answer: A) *H2O*

Explanation: The chemical formula for water is *H2O*.

69. Answer: C) Jupiter

Explanation: Jupiter is the largest planet in the Solar System.

70. Answer: C) Storing Genetic Information

Explanation: DNA (deoxyribonucleic acid) is the molecule that contains the genetic code for living organisms.

71. Answer: C) Bicep

Explanation: The bicep is the muscle in the upper arm that is used to flex the elbow.

72. Answer: D) Long-distance running

Explanation: Long-distance running helps build cardiovascular endurance, which refers to the ability of the heart and lungs to supply oxygen to the muscles during sustained physical activity. While sprinting and jump rope may improve speed and coordination, long-distance running is most closely associated with improving cardiovascular endurance.

73. Answer: B) Proteins

Explanation: Proteins are crucial for the building and repair of tissues in the body.

74. Answer: B) Providing Structure and Support

Explanation: The main function of the skeletal system is to provide structure and support to the body.

75. Answer: C) Cardiovascular Endurance

Explanation: Regular aerobic exercise improves cardiovascular endurance by strengthening the heart and improving the efficiency of the circulatory system.

76. Answer: B) Alliteration

Explanation: Alliteration is the repetition of the same consonant sound at the beginning of words.

77. Answer: C) To list topics and their page numbers

Explanation: An index is used in a non-fiction book to list topics along with the page numbers where they can be found.

78. Answer: D) Possessive

Explanation: Possessive pronouns are used to indicate ownership.

79. Answer: B) Anecdote

Explanation: An anecdote is a brief story often used to illustrate a point or support a claim.

80. Answer: C) The most exciting point

Explanation: The climax is considered the most exciting point in a story, where the main conflict reaches its peak.

81. Answer: B) Thirteenth Amendment

Explanation: The Thirteenth Amendment to the U.S. Constitution abolished slavery.

82. Answer: A) Margaret Thatcher

Explanation: Margaret Thatcher was the first female Prime Minister of the United Kingdom.

83. Answer: B) 14th-17th Centuries

Explanation: The Renaissance occurred during the 14th to 17th centuries.

84. Answer: B) A period of non-violent tension between the USA and the USSR

Explanation: The "Cold War" refers to the period of non-violent geopolitical tension between the USA and the USSR that lasted from the end of World War II until the collapse of the Soviet Union.

85. Answer: D) Paris

Explanation: Paris is the capital city of France.

86. Answer: A) 2

Explanation: Substituting *x*=2 into the equation gives *y*=3·2−4=6−4=2.

87. Answer: C) 720°

Explanation: The sum of the interior angles of a polygon with *n* sides is given by 180(*n*−2), so for a hexagon, it is 180x4=720°.

88. Answer: A) 1/2

Explanation: There are 3 even numbers out of 6 total numbers on a standard die, so the probability is 3/6=1/2.

89. Answer: C) 50°

Explanation: The sum of the angles in a triangle is 180°, so the third angle is 180°−60°−70°=50°.

90. Answer: B) $170

Explanation: A 15% discount on $200 is $30, so the sale price is $200 - $30 = $170.

91. Answer: C) Transpiration

Explanation: Transpiration is the process of water movement from the roots to the leaves of a plant, facilitated by factors like evaporation and capillary action.

92. Answer: C) NaCl

Explanation: Sodium chloride is represented by the formula NaCl.

93. Answer: B) Liquid

Explanation: Liquids have a definite volume but take the shape of their container.

94. Answer: D) Vitamin K

Explanation: Vitamin K is essential for blood clotting.

95. Answer: D) Star

Explanation: The Sun is a star, which is a luminous celestial body made mostly of hydrogen and helium.

96. Answer: B) Anaerobic

Explanation: Anaerobic exercise, such as weight lifting, focuses on increasing muscle size and strength.

97. Answer: C) Body Composition

Explanation: Body Mass Index (BMI) is used to assess a person's body composition, specifically the relationship between weight and height.

98. Answer: B) Potassium

Explanation: Potassium plays a role in regulating nerve function and fluid balance in the body.

99. Answer: A) Sprain

Explanation: A sprain is an injury to a ligament and commonly occurs from overuse or misuse of a joint.

100. Answer: A) Rest, Ice, Compression, Elevation

Explanation: "RICE" stands for Rest, Ice, Compression, Elevation, and it's a common method for treating injuries.

8.1 Full-Length Practice Test 2

Reading, Language, and Literature:

Question 101: What is the term for a word that sounds like what it describes?

A) Metaphor

B) Simile

C) Onomatopoeia

D) Alliteration

Question 102: In literature, what is a recurring symbol or motif called?

A) Theme

B) Tone

C) Allegory

D) Leitmotif

Question 103: Which type of poetry has 17 syllables arranged in three lines of 5, 7, and 5 syllables?

A) Sonnet

B) Limerick

C) Haiku

D) Free verse

Question 104: What does a semicolon primarily function to do in a sentence?

A) Separate items in a list

B) Begin a new paragraph

C) Connect closely related independent clauses

D) Mark the end of a sentence

Question 105: What is the antonym of "expand"?

A) Contract

B) Enlarge

C) Extend

D) Inflate

History and Social Science:

Question 106: The Colosseum, an ancient amphitheater, is a landmark associated with which civilization?

A) Ancient Rome

B) Ancient Persia

C) Maya Civilization

D) Inca Empire

Question 107: Who was the President of the United States during World War I?

A) Franklin D. Roosevelt

B) Woodrow Wilson

C) Abraham Lincoln

D) Thomas Jefferson

Question 108: The Berlin Wall was primarily built to prevent people from fleeing from East Berlin to where?

A) West Berlin

B) South Berlin

C) East Germany

D) West Germany

Question 109: Which African country was formerly known as Abyssinia?

A) Nigeria

B) Kenya

C) Ethiopia

D) South Africa

Question 110: What do economists use a Lorenz curve to represent?

A) Supply and demand

B) Inflation rates

C) Economic growth

D) Income distribution

Mathematics:

Question 111: What is the solution to the equation $2x-5=11$?

A) $x=3$

B) $x=8$

C) $x=-3$

D) $x=5$

Question 112: What is the area of a triangle with a base of 10 and a height of 6?

A) 30

B) 60

C) 15

D) 45

Question 113: What is the common logarithm (base 10) of 1000?

A) 2

B) 3

C) 4

D) 5

Question 114: If a circle has a radius of 5, what is its circumference?

A) 10π

B) 15π

C) 25π

D) 30π

Question 115: Which of the following numbers is irrational?

A) 1/3

B) 2/5

C) $\sqrt{3}$

D) 0.75

Science:

Question 116: Which planet is known as the "Morning Star" or the "Evening Star" and is the brightest natural object in the night sky after the Moon?

A) Venus

B) Mercury

C) Mars

D) Jupiter

Question 117: What is the term for the opening and closing of small pores on the surface of leaves, regulating gas exchange and water loss in plants?

A) Stomata

B) Chloroplasts

C) Xylem

D) Phloem

Question 118: What is the most abundant noble gas in the Earth's atmosphere?

A) Helium (He)

B) Neon (Ne)

C) Argon (Ar)

D) Krypton (Kr)

Question 119: What type of bond forms between two atoms when they share electrons?

A) Ionic bond

B) Covalent bond

C) Hydrogen bond

D) Metallic bond

Question 120: What is the scientific term for a substance that speeds up a chemical reaction without being consumed?

A) Catalyst

B) Solvent

C) Solute

D) Reactant

Physical Education and Human Development:

Question 121: What term describes the ability of a joint to move through its full range of motion?

A) Flexibility

B) Endurance

C) Strength

D) Power

Question 122: What nutrient is essential for the formation and maintenance of strong bones and teeth?

A) Vitamin C

B) Calcium

C) Iron

D) Zinc

Question 123: What type of stretching involves bouncing movements?

A) Dynamic stretching

B) Static stretching

C) Ballistic stretching

D) Passive stretching

Question 124: Which system in the body is primarily responsible for fighting infections?

A) Digestive system

B) Respiratory system

C) Immune system

D) Circulatory system

Question 125: What type of exercise emphasizes the mind-body connection and often includes meditation and breath control?

A) Weightlifting

B) Aerobics

C) Pilates

D) Yoga

Visual and Performing Arts:

Question 126: What famous artist is known for his painting "Starry Night"?

A) Pablo Picasso

B) Leonardo da Vinci

C) Vincent van Gogh

D) Salvador Dali

Question 127: In music, what term refers to the speed at which a piece is played?

A) Rhythm

B) Tempo

C) Melody

D) Harmony

Question 128: Which ballet is associated with Tchaikovsky's famous "Dance of the Sugar Plum Fairy"?

A) Romeo and Juliet

B) The Nutcracker

C) Swan Lake

D) Giselle

Question 129: What principle of art refers to the arrangement of elements to create stability in an artwork?

A) Emphasis

B) Contrast

C) Unity

D) Balance

Question 130: What genre of theater often involves exaggerated characters and situations, and is typically humorous?

A) Tragedy

B) Farce

C) Drama

D) Musical

Reading, Language, and Literature:

Question 131: In the phrase "as brave as a lion," what literary device is being used?

A) Simile

B) Metaphor

C) Alliteration

D) Personification

Question 132: In Shakespeare's "Romeo and Juliet," what family does Juliet belong to?

A) Montague

B) Capulet

C) Lancaster

D) York

Question 133: What is the main function of a thesis statement in an essay?

A) To provide a conclusion

B) To describe the main characters

C) To introduce the topic

D) To state the main argument or point

Question 134: What type of poetry does not follow specific patterns of rhyme or meter?

A) Sonnet

B) Limerick

C) Haiku

D) Free verse

Question 135: What literary term describes the time and place in which a story occurs?

A) Theme

B) Plot

C) Setting

D) Characterization

History and Social Science:

Question 136: What was the main goal of the U.S. Marshall Plan after World War II?

A) To establish military bases in Europe

B) To rebuild European economies

C) To annex territories

D) To encourage communism

Question 137: Who succeeded David Cameron as the leader of the Conservative Party and became Prime Minister in 2016?

A) Theresa May

B) Boris Johnson

C) Michael Gove

D) Andrea Leadsom

Question 138: What was the main purpose of the Berlin Airlift (1948–1949)?

A) To transport weapons to West Berlin

B) To deliver food and supplies to West Berlin

C) To evacuate civilians from East Berlin

D) To establish air superiority over Berlin

History and Social Science:

Question 139: Which U.S. President signed the Emancipation Proclamation?

A) Abraham Lincoln

B) George Washington

C) Thomas Jefferson

D) Andrew Jackson

Question 140: What was the primary objective of the Women's Suffrage movement in the early 20th century in the United States?

A) To gain equal pay for women

B) To grant women the right to vote

C) To promote women in politics

D) To encourage women's education

Mathematics:

Question 141: What is the value of x in the equation $2x+4=12$?

A) 2

B) 3

C) 4

D) 5

Question 142: What term describes a polygon with all sides and angles equal?

A) Isosceles

B) Scalene

C) Regular

D) Irregular

Question 143: If $y=3x$, what is the value of y when $x=5$?

A) 10

B) 15

C) 20

D) 25

Question 144: What is the slope of the line defined by the equation $y=-2x+5$?

A) -2

B) 0

C) 2

D) 5

Question 145: What is the area of a circle with a radius of 4 units?

A) 8π

B) 12π

C) 16π

D) 32π

Science:

Question 146: Which process involves the transport of sugars produced during photosynthesis from the leaves to other parts of the plant?

A) Transpiration

B) Respiration

C) Translocation

D) Germination

Question 147: Which planet is distinguished by its prominent ring system?

A) Jupiter

B) Saturn

C) Uranus

D) Neptune

Question 148: What is the chemical symbol for mercury?

A) Mg

B) Hg

C) Mn

D) Mo

Question 149: Which type of wave requires a medium to travel?

A) Sound waves

B) Light waves

C) Microwaves

D) X-rays

Question 150: What is the process by which liquid water changes into water vapor?

A) Condensation

B) Evaporation

C) Freezing

D) Melting

Physical Education and Human Development:

Question 151: What is the primary source of energy for immediate, short-term bursts of activity?

A) Fats

B) Carbohydrates

C) Proteins

D) ATP

Question 152: What type of joint allows for movement in all directions?

A) Hinge joint

B) Pivot joint

C) Ball-and-socket joint

D) Gliding joint

Question 153: What component of fitness refers to the ability to use strength quickly?

A) Flexibility

B) Power

C) Endurance

D) Balance

Question 154: What vitamin is primarily responsible for aiding in the absorption of calcium?

A) Vitamin A

B) Vitamin B

C) Vitamin C

D) Vitamin D

Question 155: What BMI range is generally considered as "Normal" or healthy weight?

A) Below 18.5

B) 18.5 - 24.9

C) 25 - 29.9

D) 30 and above

Reading, Language, and Literature:

Question 156: What part of a story typically introduces the characters, setting, and initial conflict?

A) Climax

B) Exposition

C) Rising Action

D) Resolution

Question 157: Who wrote the epic poem "The Odyssey"?

A) Homer

B) Dante

C) Shakespeare

D) Virgil

Question 158: What is the term for a word that is spelled and pronounced the same forward and backward, like "racecar"?

A) Anagram

B) Acronym

C) Palindrome

D) Homophone

Question 159: What is a haiku?

A) A 14-line poem with a specific rhyme scheme

B) A 3-line poem with a 5-7-5 syllable pattern

C) A 4-line poem with an ABAB rhyme scheme

D) A 5-line poem with a humorous tone

Question 160: What is the antonym of "vivid"?

A) Dull

B) Lively

C) Bright

D) Colorful

History and Social Science:

Question 161: Who was the President of the United States during the Great Depression and World War II?

A) Franklin D. Roosevelt

B) Herbert Hoover

C) Calvin Coolidge

D) Harry S. Truman

Question 162: What was the primary cause of World War I?

A) The assassination of Archduke Franz Ferdinand

B) The bombing of Pearl Harbor

C) The Great Depression

D) The Treaty of Versailles

Question 163: What economic system emphasizes collective or governmental ownership and administration of the means of production?

A) Capitalism

B) Socialism

C) Mercantilism

D) Feudalism

Question 164: Who was the Egyptian queen known for her relationship with Roman leaders Julius Caesar and Mark Antony?

A) Nefertiti

B) Cleopatra

C) Hatshepsut

D) Sheba

Question 165: What was the main purpose of the Monroe Doctrine?

A) To abolish slavery

B) To prevent European colonization in the Americas

C) To establish the U.S. banking system

D) To declare independence from Britain

Mathematics:

Question 166: If a triangle has angles of 30°, 60°, and 90°, what type of triangle is it?

A) Isosceles

B) Equilateral

C) Right

D) Scalene

Question 167: What is the solution to the inequality $5x-3 \geq 7$?

A) $x \geq 2$

B) $x \leq 2$

C) $x \geq 3$

D) $x \leq 3$

Question 168: If a line has a slope of 0, what type of line is it?

A) Vertical

B) Horizontal

C) Diagonal

D) None of the above

Question 169: What is the midpoint of the line segment with endpoints (4, 6) and (6, 8)?

A) (3, 5)

B) (4, 6)

C) (4, 4)

D) (5, 7)

Question 170: What is the sum of the first 5 positive even numbers?

A) 20

B) 25

C) 30

D) 35

Science:

Question 171: What is the largest organ in the human body?

A) Heart

B) Brain

C) Liver

D) Skin

Question 172: Which part of a plant is responsible for absorbing water and minerals from the soil?

A) Leaves

B) Flowers

C) Roots

D) Stems

Question 173: What is the primary function of red blood cells?

A) Fighting infection

B) Clotting blood

C) Carrying oxygen

D) Regulating body temperature

Question 174: In which phase of matter do particles have the least energy and are arranged in a regular, fixed pattern?

A) Solid

B) Liquid

C) Gas

D) Plasma

Question 175: What planet is known for its Great Red Spot, a giant storm?

A) Venus

B) Mars

C) Jupiter

D) Saturn

Physical Education and Human Development:

Question 176: What type of joint allows for rotation, such as turning the head?

A) Ball and socket

B) Hinge

C) Pivot

D) Saddle

Question 177: Which nutrient is known for its antioxidant properties and is essential for immune function and skin health?

A) Vitamin D

B) Vitamin E

C) Vitamin K

D) Vitamin B12

Question 178: In the context of physical education, what does the acronym BMI stand for?

A) Body Mass Index

B) Basal Metabolic Indicator

C) Body Muscle Indicator

D) Balanced Movement Instruction

Question 179: What is the name of the process where bones become more fragile and likely to fracture, often occurring in older adults?

A) Arthritis

B) Osteoporosis

C) Tendonitis

D) Scoliosis

Question 180: What is the recommended amount of physical activity for children aged 6–17, according to the U.S. Department of Health and Human Services?

A) 30 minutes per day

B) 1 hour per day

C) 2 hours per day

D) 3 hours per day

Visual and Performing Arts:

Question 181: What style of painting is characterized by small, distinct dots of color that are applied in patterns to form an image?

A) Cubism

B) Pointillism

C) Surrealism

D) Abstract Expressionism

Question 182: What musical period followed the Baroque period and emphasized clarity, order, and balance?

A) Romantic

B) Classical

C) Renaissance

D) Modern

Question 183: In theater, what term refers to the imaginary barrier that separates the audience from the performers?

A) Fourth Wall

B) Curtain Line

C) Stage Left

D) Downstage

Question 184: Which of the following instruments is a member of the wood-wind family?

A) Trumpet

B) Violin

C) Flute

D) Cello

Question 185: Who is the famous ballet dancer known for defecting from the Soviet Union to the West in 1961?

A) Mikhail Baryshnikov

B) George Balanchine

C) Rudolf Nureyev

D) Margot Fonteyn

Literature and Language Arts:

Question 186: In which novel does the character Atticus Finch appear?

A) "To Kill a Mockingbird"

B) "The Catcher in the Rye"

C) "Moby-Dick"

D) "Pride and Prejudice"

Question 187: What type of poetic meter consists of five pairs of unstressed and stressed syllables?

A) Tetrameter

B) Pentameter

C) Hexameter

D) Octameter

Question 188: Who is the author of "One Hundred Years of Solitude"?

A) Gabriel García Márquez

B) Ernest Hemingway

C) F. Scott Fitzgerald

D) George Orwell

Technology and Computer Science:

Question 189: What is the primary function of a computer's CPU?

A) Storing data

B) Displaying graphics

C) Processing instructions

D) Connecting to the internet

Question 190: What programming language is known for its use in web development and runs on the client side?

A) Python

B) Java

C) JavaScript

D) C++

Geography:

Question 191: What is the capital of Brazil?

A) Rio de Janeiro

B) Buenos Aires

C) Brasília

D) São Paulo

Question 192: What body of water separates Saudi Arabia and Africa?

A) Red Sea

B) Indian Ocean

C) Arabian Sea

D) Persian Gulf

Question 193: Which country is known as the Land of the Rising Sun?

A) China

B) Japan

C) South Korea

D) India

Environmental Science:

Question 194: What type of energy is derived from the Earth's internal heat?

A) Solar Energy

B) Wind Energy

C) Geothermal Energy

D) Hydroelectric Energy

Question 195: What is the main gas responsible for the greenhouse effect in the Earth's atmosphere?

A) Oxygen

B) Nitrogen

C) Carbon Dioxide

D) Helium

Health Education:

Question 196: What vitamin is produced in the skin in response to sunlight?

A) Vitamin A

B) Vitamin C

C) Vitamin D

D) Vitamin E

Question 197: What organ is responsible for detoxifying chemicals and metabolizing drugs in the body?

A) Heart

B) Liver

C) Kidneys

D) Pancreas

Question 198: What is the medical term for high blood pressure?

A) Hypothyroidism

B) Hypertension

C) Hyperglycemia

D) Hyperextension

Question 199: What type of fat is considered unhealthy and found in many processed foods?

A) Unsaturated Fat

B) Saturated Fat

C) Trans Fat

D) Polyunsaturated Fat

Question 200: What is the body's largest internal organ?

A) Heart

B) Liver

C) Lungs

D) Kidneys

8.2 ANSWER SHEET - PRACTICE TEST 2

101. Answer: C) Onomatopoeia

Explanation: Onomatopoeia refers to a word that sounds like what it describes, such as "buzz" or "crack."

102. Answer: D) Leitmotif

Explanation: A leitmotif is a recurring theme, symbol, or motif in a literary work.

103. Answer: C) Haiku

Explanation: A haiku is a form of Japanese poetry consisting of 17 syllables arranged in three lines of 5, 7, and 5 syllables.

104. Answer: C) Connect closely related independent clauses

Explanation: A semicolon is used to connect closely related independent clauses within a sentence.

105. Answer: A) Contract

Explanation: "Expand" and "Contract" are antonyms, representing opposite actions related to size or volume.

106. Answer: A) Ancient Rome

Explanation: The Colosseum is a symbol of ancient Roman engineering and is located in the heart of Rome.

107. Answer: B) Woodrow Wilson

Explanation: Woodrow Wilson was the President of the United States during World War I.

108. Answer: A) West Berlin

Explanation: The Berlin Wall was built to prevent people from fleeing from East Berlin to West Berlin.

109. Answer: C) Ethiopia

Explanation: Ethiopia was formerly known as Abyssinia.

110. Answer: D) Income distribution

Explanation: A Lorenz curve is a graphical representation of the distribution of income within a population.

111. Answer: B) $x=8$

Explanation: To solve the equation $2x-5=11$, you can add 5 to both sides to get $2x=16$, and then divide by 2 to solve for x, giving you $x=8$.

112. Answer: A) 30

Explanation: The area of a triangle is given by 1/2×base×height, so the area is 1/2×10×6=30.

113. Answer: B) 3

Explanation: The common logarithm of 1000 is 3 since 103=1000.

114. Answer: A) 10π

Explanation: The circumference of a circle is given by $2\pi r$, so the circumference is $2\pi \times 5 = 10\pi$.

115. Answer: C) √3

Explanation: √3 is an irrational number, meaning it cannot be expressed as a simple fraction.

116. Answer: A) Venus

Explanation: Venus is often called the "Morning Star" or the "Evening Star" and is the brightest natural object in the night sky after the Moon.

117. Answer: A) Stomata

Explanation: Stomata are small pores on the surface of leaves that open and close to regulate gas exchange (including CO2 intake for photosynthesis) and water loss.

118. Answer: C) Argon (Ar)

Explanation: Argon is the most abundant noble gas in the Earth's atmosphere.

119. Answer: B) Covalent bond

Explanation: A covalent bond forms when two atoms share electrons.

120. Answer: A) Catalyst

Explanation: A catalyst is a substance that speeds up a chemical reaction without being consumed in the reaction.

121. Answer: A) Flexibility

Explanation: Flexibility is the ability of a joint to move through its full range of motion.

122. Answer: B) Calcium

Explanation: Calcium is crucial for the formation and maintenance of strong bones and teeth.

123. Answer: C) Ballistic stretching

Explanation: Ballistic stretching involves bouncing movements and is typically used to warm up muscles before exercise.

124. Answer: C) Immune system

Explanation: The immune system is primarily responsible for fighting infections in the body.

125. Answer: D) Yoga

Explanation: Yoga emphasizes the mind-body connection and often includes practices such as meditation and breath control.

126. Answer: C) Vincent van Gogh

Explanation: "Starry Night" is one of Vincent van Gogh's most famous paintings.

127. Answer: B) Tempo

Explanation: Tempo refers to the speed at which a piece of music is played.

128. Answer: B) The Nutcracker

Explanation: "Dance of the Sugar Plum Fairy" is a part of Tchaikovsky's ballet "The Nutcracker."

129. Answer: D) Balance

Explanation: Balance refers to the arrangement of elements in an artwork to create stability.

130. Answer: B) Farce

Explanation: Farce is a genre of theater that often involves exaggerated characters and situations, and is typically humorous.

131. Answer: A) Simile

Explanation: A simile makes a comparison using "like" or "as," as seen in "as brave as a lion."

132. Answer: B) Capulet

Explanation: In "Romeo and Juliet," Juliet is a member of the Capulet family.

133. Answer: D) To state the main argument or point

Explanation: The thesis statement in an essay is used to state the main argument or point that the essay will support.

134. Answer: D) Free verse

Explanation: Free verse is a type of poetry that does not follow specific patterns of rhyme or meter.

135. Answer: C) Setting

Explanation: The setting of a story refers to the time and place in which it occurs.

136. Answer: B) To rebuild European economies

Explanation: The Marshall Plan was implemented to help rebuild European economies after World War II.

137. Answer: A) Theresa May

Explanation: Theresa May succeeded David Cameron as the leader of the Conservative Party and became Prime Minister in 2016.

138. Answer: B) To deliver food and supplies to West Berlin

Explanation: The Berlin Airlift was conducted to deliver food and supplies to West Berlin when land routes were blocked by the Soviet Union.

139. Answer: A) Abraham Lincoln

Explanation: Abraham Lincoln signed the Emancipation Proclamation in 1863, declaring that all slaves in Confederate territory were to be set free.

140. Answer: B) To grant women the right to vote

Explanation: The primary objective of the Women's Suffrage movement in the early 20th century was to gain voting rights for women, leading to the passage of the 19th Amendment in 1920.

141. Answer: C) 4

Explanation: Subtracting 4 from both sides gives $2x=8$, and then dividing by 2 gives $x=4$.

142. Answer: C) Regular

Explanation: A regular polygon has all sides and angles equal.

143. Answer: B) 15

Explanation: Substituting $x=5$ into the equation $y=3x$ gives $y=15$.

144. Answer: A) -2

Explanation: The slope of the line given by $y=mx+b$ is the coefficient of x, which is -2 in this case.

145. Answer: C) 16π

Explanation: The area of a circle is given by $\pi r2$, so the area is 16π when the radius is 4.

146. Answer: C) Translocation

Explanation: Translocation is the process of transporting sugars, produced during photosynthesis, from the leaves to other parts of the plant for growth and energy storage.

147. Answer: B) Saturn

- **Explanation**: Saturn is known for its stunning ring system, making it easily distinguishable.

148. Answer: B) Hg

- **Explanation**: The chemical symbol for mercury is Hg.

149. Answer: A) Sound waves

Explanation: Sound waves require a medium (such as air, water, or solids) to travel.

150. Answer: B) Evaporation

Explanation: Evaporation is the process by which liquid water changes into water vapor.

151. Answer: D) ATP

Explanation: Adenosine triphosphate (ATP) is the primary source of energy for immediate, short-term bursts of activity.

152. Answer: C) Ball-and-socket joint

Explanation: Ball-and-socket joints, such as the hip and shoulder joints, allow for movement in all directions.

153. Answer: B) Power

Explanation: Power refers to the ability to use strength quickly and is a key component of fitness.

154. Answer: D) Vitamin D

Explanation: Vitamin D aids in the absorption of calcium, which is essential for bone health.

155. Answer: B) 18.5 - 24.9

Explanation: A BMI within the range of 18.5 to 24.9 is generally considered as "Normal" or healthy weight.

156. Answer: B) Exposition

Explanation: The exposition is the beginning of the story that introduces essential elements like characters, setting, and the initial conflict.

157. Answer: A) Homer

Explanation: "The Odyssey" is an ancient Greek epic poem attributed to the poet Homer.

158. Answer: C) Palindrome

Explanation: A palindrome is a word, phrase, number, or other sequences of characters that reads the same forward and backward (ignoring spaces, punctuation, and capitalization).

159. Answer: B) A 3-line poem with a 5-7-5 syllable pattern

Explanation: A haiku is a traditional form of Japanese poetry consisting of three lines, with a 5-7-5 syllable pattern.

160. Answer: A) Dull

Explanation: "Vivid" and "Dull" are antonyms, representing opposite levels of brightness or intensity.

161. Answer: A) Franklin D. Roosevelt

Explanation: Franklin D. Roosevelt was the President during the Great Depression and World War II.

162. Answer: A) The assassination of Archduke Franz Ferdinand

Explanation: The assassination of Archduke Franz Ferdinand of Austria-Hungary set off a series of events that led to the outbreak of World War I.

163. Answer: B) Socialism

Explanation: Socialism emphasizes collective or governmental ownership and administration of the means of production and distribution of goods.

164. Answer: B) Cleopatra

Explanation: Cleopatra was the last ruler of the Ptolemaic Kingdom of Egypt, known for her relationships with Roman leaders Julius Caesar and Mark Antony.

165. Answer: B) To prevent European colonization in the Americas

Explanation: The Monroe Doctrine was a policy stating that further efforts by European nations to colonize or interfere with states in North or South America would be viewed as acts of aggression.

166. Answer: C) Right

Explanation: A triangle with angles of 30°, 60°, and 90° is a right triangle because one of its angles is 90°.

167. Answer: A) $x \geq 2$

Explanation: By adding 3 to both sides and then dividing by 5, we get $x \geq 2$.

168. Answer: B) Horizontal

Explanation: A line with a slope of 0 is horizontal.

169. Answer: D) (5, 7)

Explanation: The midpoint of a line segment with endpoints $(x1, y1)$ and $(x2, y2)$ is $(x1+x2/2, y1+y2/2)$, which in this case is (5, 7).

170. Answer: C) 30

Explanation: The sum of the first 5 positive even numbers (2 + 4 + 6 + 8 + 10) is 30.

171. Answer: D) Skin

Explanation: The skin is the largest organ in the human body.

172. Answer: C) Roots

Explanation: The roots of a plant are responsible for absorbing water and minerals from the soil.

173. Answer: C) Carrying oxygen

Explanation: The primary function of red blood cells is to carry oxygen to body tissues.

174. Answer: A) Solid

Explanation: In the solid phase, particles have the least energy and are arranged in a regular, fixed pattern.

175. Answer: C) Jupiter

Explanation: Jupiter's Great Red Spot is a massive storm that has been raging for hundreds of years.

176. Answer: C) Pivot

Explanation: A pivot joint allows for rotation around a single axis, such as turning the head.

177. Answer: B) Vitamin E

Explanation: Vitamin E is an antioxidant nutrient essential for immune function and skin health.

178. Answer: A) Body Mass Index

Explanation: BMI stands for Body Mass Index, which is a measure of body fat based on height and weight.

179. Answer: B) Osteoporosis

Explanation: Osteoporosis is a condition that weakens bones, making them fragile and more likely to break.

180. Answer: B) 1 hour per day

Explanation: The U.S. Department of Health and Human Services recommends at least 1 hour of physical activity per day for children aged 6–17.

181. Answer: B) Pointillism

Explanation: Pointillism is characterized by small, distinct dots of color applied in patterns to form an image.

182. Answer: B) Classical

Explanation: The Classical period in music followed the Baroque period, emphasizing clarity, order, and balance.

183. Answer: A) Fourth Wall

Explanation: The term "Fourth Wall" refers to the imaginary barrier that separates the audience from the performers in a theater.

184. Answer: C) Flute

Explanation: The flute is a member of the woodwind family of musical instruments.

185. Answer: C) Rudolf Nureyev

Explanation: Rudolf Nureyev was a famous ballet dancer known for defecting from the Soviet Union to the West in 1961.

186. Answer: A) "To Kill a Mockingbird"

Explanation: Atticus Finch is a character in Harper Lee's novel "To Kill a Mockingbird."

187. Answer: B) Pentameter

Explanation: Pentameter consists of five pairs of unstressed and stressed syllables.

188. Answer: A) Gabriel García Márquez

Explanation: Gabriel García Márquez is the author of "One Hundred Years of Solitude."

189. Answer: C) Processing instructions

Explanation: The primary function of a computer's CPU (Central Processing Unit) is to process instructions.

190. Answer: C) JavaScript

Explanation: JavaScript is a programming language used in web development and runs on the client side.

191. Answer: C) Brasília

Explanation: Brasília is the capital of Brazil.

192. Answer: A) Red Sea

Explanation: The Red Sea separates Saudi Arabia and Africa.

193. Answer: B) Japan

Explanation: Japan is known as the Land of the Rising Sun.

194. Answer: C) Geothermal Energy

Explanation: Geothermal energy is derived from the Earth's internal heat.

195. Answer: C) Carbon Dioxide

Explanation: Carbon dioxide is the main gas responsible for the greenhouse effect in the Earth's atmosphere.

196. Answer: C) Vitamin D

Explanation: Vitamin D is produced in the skin in response to sunlight.

197. Answer: B) Liver

Explanation: The liver is responsible for detoxifying chemicals and metabolizing drugs in the body.

198. Answer: B) Hypertension

Explanation: Hypertension is the medical term for high blood pressure.

199. Answer: C) Trans Fat

Explanation: Trans fat is considered unhealthy and is found in many processed foods.

200. Answer: B) Liver

Explanation: The liver is the body's largest internal organ.

TEST-TAKING STRATEGIES

As you stand on the threshold of the CSET exam, equipped with knowledge and preparation, it's essential to complement your expertise with effective test-taking strategies and techniques to conquer any nerves that may arise. This section provides you with insights to navigate the exam confidently and overcome test anxiety.

1. Understand the Question Styles:

Familiarize yourself with the different question styles you'll encounter on the CSET exam, including multiple-choice and constructed-response questions. Read questions carefully, focusing on keywords and the specific information being sought. Pay attention to qualifiers such as "not," "except," and "most likely."

2. Time Management:

Time is your most valuable resource during the exam. Allocate a specific amount of time to each question based on its complexity. If you're uncertain about an answer, flag it and move on to ensure you maximize your points within the allocated time.

3. Constructed-Response Mastery:

For constructed-response questions, follow a structured approach. Begin with a concise introduction that outlines your response's main points. Provide detailed explanations supported by examples and evidence. Conclude by summarizing your key arguments. A well-organized response enhances your clarity and boosts your score.

4. Process of Elimination:

When faced with multiple-choice questions, employ the process of elimination. Eliminate obviously incorrect options to narrow down your choices. This increases your likelihood of selecting the correct answer, even if you're unsure.

5. Prioritize Confidence:

Answer questions you're confident about first, then return to more challenging ones. Prioritizing questions you know will earn you points without wasting time on uncertainty.

6. Manage Test Anxiety:

Test anxiety is common but manageable. Practice relaxation techniques such as deep breathing, visualization, and positive affirmations. Remind yourself that you've prepared diligently and are capable of success.

7. Simulate Exam Conditions:

During practice tests, create an environment that mimics the actual exam. Sit in a quiet space, adhere to time constraints, and maintain focus. This helps you become accustomed to the pressure and conditions you'll face on exam day.

8. Review and Revise:

Allocate time at the end to review your answers. Verify that you've answered all questions, and revisit flagged items. Check for careless errors and ensure your responses are clear and concise.

9. Trust Your Instincts:

When unsure about an answer, trust your intuition. Often, your initial instinct is correct. Avoid overthinking or second-guessing yourself.

10. Reflect on Progress:

After each practice test, reflect on your performance. Identify areas of strength and weakness, and adjust your study plan accordingly. Consistently refining your approach enhances your overall readiness.

Remember, the CSET exam is not only a test of knowledge but also a demonstration of your ability to apply your understanding effectively. By implementing these strategies and addressing test anxiety, you're positioning yourself for success. With confidence, preparation, and a strategic mindset, you're poised to excel and embark on your journey towards becoming an outstanding educator.

Additional Resources

As you embark on your journey to prepare for the Pharmacy Technician Certification Board (PTCB) Exam, we understand the value of having a variety of resources at your disposal. In this section, we've compiled a list of recommended online resources and academic materials that complement our study guide and enhance your preparation experience.

Recommended Online Resources:

1. **PTCB Official Website (www.ptcb.org):** The official website of the Pharmacy Technician Certification Board offers valuable information about the exam, including exam content, registration details, and resources for candidates.

2. **Khan Academy (www.khanacademy.org):** Khan Academy provides free courses on a wide range of subjects, including pharmacy-related topics. Their interactive lessons can reinforce your understanding of key concepts.

3. **Pharmacy Times (www.pharmacytimes.com):** This reputable platform offers news, articles, and insights related to pharmacy practice, medications, and healthcare trends. Stay informed about the latest developments in the field.

4. **American Pharmacists Association (www.pharmacist.com):** Ex-

plore resources, publications, and educational materials from a leading organization in the pharmacy industry. Their content covers various aspects of pharmacy practice.

5. **YouTube Educational Channels:** Numerous YouTube channels offer instructional videos on pharmacy topics. Search for reliable channels that provide clear explanations and visual aids.

Recommended Academic Materials:

1. **"Mosby's Pharmacy Technician Exam Review" by James J. Mizner:** This comprehensive review book offers practice questions and explanations to help you reinforce your knowledge and test-taking skills.

2. **"Pharmacy Technician Certification Exam Review" by Cheryl Aiken:** Dive into a comprehensive review of pharmacy technician concepts, practice exams, and detailed answer explanations.

3. **"Pharmacy Technician Certification Quick-Study Guide" by Kristy Malacos:** This compact guide provides concise summaries of essential pharmacy topics, making it a handy reference for quick revision.

4. **"Pharmacy Technician Exam Certification and Review" by Jodi Dreiling and Lynette R. Bradley-Baker:** This resource combines review material with practice questions to aid your exam preparation.

5. **"Top 200 Drugs Flashcards" by Tony Guerra:** Reinforce your medication knowledge with flashcards that cover the top 200 drugs frequently encountered in pharmacy practice.

These recommended online resources and academic materials complement our study guide, offering you a diverse range of learning tools to enhance your understanding and preparation for the PTCB Exam. Feel free to explore these resources to tailor your learning experience and boost your confidence as you approach the exam.

Best regards.

Explore Our Range of Study Guides

At Test Treasure Publication, we understand that academic success requires more than just raw intelligence or tireless effort—it requires targeted preparation. That's why we offer an extensive range of study guides, meticulously designed to help you excel in various exams across the USA.

Our Offerings

- **Medical Exams:** Conquer the MCAT, USMLE, and more with our comprehensive study guides, complete with practice questions and diagnostic tests.

- **Law Exams:** Get a leg up on the LSAT and bar exams with our tailored resources, offering theoretical insights and practical exercises.

- **Business and Management Tests:** Ace the GMAT and other business exams with our incisive guides, equipped with real-world examples and scenarios.

- **Engineering & Technical Exams:** Prep for the FE, PE, and other technical exams with our specialized guides, which delve into both fundamentals and complexities.

- **High School Exams:** Be it the SAT, ACT, or AP tests, our high school range is designed to give you a competitive edge.

- **State-Specific Exams:** Tailored resources to help you with exams unique to specific states, whether it's teacher qualification exams or state civil service exams.

Why Choose Test Treasure Publication?

- **Comprehensive Coverage:** Each guide covers all essential topics in detail.

- **Quality Material:** Crafted by experts in each field.

- **Interactive Tools:** Flashcards, online quizzes, and downloadable resources to complement your study.

- **Customizable Learning:** Personalize your prep journey by focusing on areas where you need the most help.

- **Community Support:** Access to online forums where you can discuss concerns, seek guidance, and share success stories.

Contact Us

For inquiries about our study guides, or to provide feedback, please email us at support@testtreasure.com.

Order Now

Ready to elevate your preparation to the next level? Visit our website www.testtreasure.com to browse our complete range of study guides and make your purchase.

Made in the USA
Coppell, TX
23 January 2025